WHAT NOW?

What now?

A handbook for NEW PARENTS

Mary Lou Rozdilsky
and Barbara Banet

Illustrations by
Lily Freemountain

Charles Scribner's Sons, New York

Library of Congress Cataloging in Publication Data

Rozdilsky, Mary Lou
  What now?

  Bibliography: p.
  Includes index.
    1. Puerperium. 2. Infants (Newborn)—Care and
hygiene. 3. Parent and child. I. Banet, Barbara
joint author. II. Title.
RG801.B23   649'.122   75-17669
ISBN 0-684-14382-8 (cloth)
ISBN 0-684-14698-3 (paper)

Grateful acknowledgment is made for permission to reprint the following:

Pages 56 and 67, reprinted from Redbook Magazine, June 1974.
Copyright © 1974, The Redbook Publishing Company.

Pages 58, 66 and 72, copyright © 1945, 1946 by Benjamin Spock, M.D.,
© 1957, 1958 by Benjamin Spock, M.D. Reprinted by permission of
Pocket Books, a division of Simon & Schuster, Inc.

Pages 68 and 69–70, from Your Child Is a Person by Stella Chess, M.D.,
Alexander Thomas, M.D. and Herbert G. Birch, M.D., Ph.D. Copyright ©
1965 Dr. Stella Chess, Dr. Alexander Thomas, and Dr. Herbert G. Birch.
Reprinted by permission of The Viking Press.

Page 99 from Giving Birth: The Parents' Emotions in Childbirth by Sheila
Kitzinger. Copyright © 1971 by Sheila Kitzinger. Reprinted by permission
of Taplinger Publishing Co.

Page 104, from Becoming Partners: Marriage and Its Alternatives by Carl R.
Rogers. Copyright © 1972 Carl R. Rogers. Reprinted by permission of
Delacorte Press.

11 13 15 17 19 F/P 20 18 16 14 12

Contents

Preface

There are many books on pregnancy and childbirth, but those that are written about the period after childbirth tend to focus, almost without exception, on the baby. Many parents interpret this to mean that they should make this major adjustment in life magically, that parenthood comes naturally and without difficulty. The social and personal attitudes that often surround new parents reinforce this impression.

This book grew out of our concern, as new mothers, for the lack of easily available information about the physical and emotional facts of life that a new mother faces. In talking with other mothers we were relieved to discover that they shared our concerns, and we realized how much guilt and uneasiness can come from feeling you are alone in what you are experiencing. With the hope of reaching other women who had recently had babies, we wrote the handbook on which this one is based, and began distributing it in September of 1972.

The response to our initial handbook has been very exciting. Hospitals and parent education groups of all sorts are ordering it in bulk, childbirth groups are including it with their materials, and new parents from around the country are writing for copies. Groups of new parents are getting together to give each other support and talk about their feelings. Both individuals and groups report a sense of relief at having a chance to share their problems with others who are making similar adjustments.

The positive responses we have received from so many readers have encouraged us to expand the first edition and to broaden its focus. We are increasingly aware of the importance of exploring the feelings and problems of new fathers as well as new mothers. Men have conflicts of their own to resolve, and they are affected by every aspect of the adjustment to parenthood. As new opportunities open up for men and women to share baby care as well as outside commitments, we feel strongly that our revised handbook should be addressed to both new parents. The real possibilities for a new family unfold only when both parents are open to involvement in all aspects of living together and can change to meet the needs that emerge.

We are also more aware of the wide range of differences in temperament that exists among babies from the moment of birth. In our revised handbook we have put more emphasis on individual differences among all family members. We recognize that all families must find their own balance of needs and priorities.

We have tried to be honest about the obstacles new parents face. Without implying that every couple finds parenthood a difficult adjustment, we have suggested solutions to some of the problems that may arise. But our handbook is necessarily limited in scope. It assumes, for example, a two-parent family because that has been the experience of both authors. We have not tried to deal with the special problems that arise when a baby dies or is born with physical difficulties, when a parent becomes very ill, when parents separate, and so on. Clearly there is a need for much more discussion of these and other problems. We urge others to write of their experiences.

It is our hope that this revised handbook will continue to encourage both parents and professionals to take the needs of the postpartum time seriously and that it will stimulate them to find ways of offering services to support new parents.

In writing the handbook we struggled with the problem of choosing pronouns to refer to babies and doctors. We find ourselves joining others who deplore the lack of pronouns that include both sexes. Throughout the book, we have used the feminine pronoun when referring to a baby and the masculine pronoun when referring to a doctor. As far as we are concerned the choice is an arbitrary and annoying compromise, made only for the sake of readability.

February 1975   *Mary Lou Rozdilsky*
                                            Barbara Banet

Acknowledgments

To the many parents who have contributed to this handbook, we wish to express our thanks. We are especially grateful to those who read the manuscript and made helpful suggestions: Bernard Banet, Susan Earley, Susan Z. Eisinger, Elsa Galbraith, Jane C. Gilbert, Paula Puma, Lyn Rabinovitch, Libby Sinclair, and Marjorie E. Wright. The following doctors advised us on the medical aspects of the book and made other helpful suggestions: Eli G. Dayton, M.D., Steven H. Eisinger, M.D., and Marvin E. Schrock, M.D. For invaluable help with "Coping with a Crying Baby," thanks to Holly A. Ruff. For her ideas on how to combine nursing and returning to work we are grateful to Rosemary Cogan. Those who helped with "Feeling Comfortable as Parents" were Paul and Louise Chernin, Bob Crittendon, Tom Galbraith, Mike McKeag, and Tony Puma. While we are greatly indebted to these people for their suggestions, we wish to make it clear that the authors take full responsibility for the final content of the handbook.

Angela Barron McBride (author of *The Growth and Development of Mothers*) urged us to address the revised book to men as well as to women and made some valuable suggestions to that end. Sheila Kitzinger (author of *The Experience of Childbirth* and other books on childbirth, childbirth preparation, and articles on sex in pregnancy and after delivery) has influenced us by her awareness of the sexual aspect of pregnancy, childbirth, and postpartum and her broad approach to the significance of the birth experience in the life of a family.

Special thanks to Elsa Galbraith for typing the manuscript and for her help with details, which has greatly improved the final manuscript.

WHAT NOW?

1

Recovering from the Birth

YOU ARE ALL RECOVERING

The first few weeks after the birth of a baby are an unexpected challenge to most new parents. For all three of you a major event has occurred, and the period ahead calls for a good deal of adjustment on everyone's part. Even if you are feeling proud and elated, you may suddenly be overwhelmed by how much is being demanded of you. The baby's care is no small task, and there are endless household and personal needs to attend to as well. New mothers often find they aren't as strong as they had anticipated and feel very tired and uncomfortable. New fathers sometimes feel more uneasy than they expected about the many changes that parenthood brings. The situation seems to call for the best you can give it, but physically and emotionally you may both feel let down and exhausted.

You may have feelings about the baby that you hadn't anticipated. Many new parents do. The baby may look very different than you had imagined and may not seem like *your* baby right away. You may not feel the kind of instant, unqualified love for your child that you expected to feel. The awkwardness that many new parents feel at handling and comforting a newborn baby also adds strain. You may at times feel unsure, lonely, or resentful. While these feelings usually don't last very long, they do add to the confusion and uncertainty of the first few weeks.

Both of you are probably wondering how long it takes a new mother to regain her energy and feel like herself again. The answer depends in part on how much rest she is able to get during the first month or so. It can be distressing for a woman to feel so tired and dependent, even if she knows that such feelings will not last forever. At times a new father may wonder whether he will have to keep the family going single-handedly.

As eager as he is for his wife to rest and recover, he may look forward to the time when she needs less help from him. Both of you may alternate between feeling that you are doing too much and worrying that you are doing too little.

Another important concern you probably share is an uncertainty about the future of your sex life. How long does it take for the mother's genital area to heal, and when will it be possible to resume intercourse? Will you both feel as attracted to each other as before? Expressing affection for each other and satisfying your sexual needs is as important now as ever, but how can you find the energy when one or both of you are feeling so overwhelmed and tired? At times you may wonder whether you have given up sex for this lovable but demanding infant.

As the two of you are struggling to meet the demands of your new situation, your infant, too, is making major adjustments to the outside world. During these first few days and weeks your baby's heartbeat, breathing, and digesting are stabilizing. For a while you will notice that she startles easily, sleeps restlessly, and sneezes frequently. Gradually, with cuddling and care from you, your infant will establish a rhythm of sleeping and waking and will become more predictable in response to the environment. But her adjustment is bound to take time and may require a lot of patience and effort on your part.

As puzzling and difficult as this period is for all of you, it is a realistic introduction to the kinds of conflicts and uncertainties you will continue to live with as a family. Admitting and communicating your changing feelings, needs, and limitations may be difficult, but by doing so you will be well on your way toward developing a comfortable sense of yourselves as parents.

THE WOMAN'S PHYSICAL RECOVERY FROM CHILDBIRTH

Consider What You've Been Through
The feelings of pride and accomplishment that often follow the birth of a baby are well-earned. In fact, some women feel

so exhilarated by the experience and are so eager to share it with others that advice to limit visitors and activities for a while may at first seem misplaced. Whether you feel ecstatic, or let down and exhausted, it is extremely important that you sit down for a minute and take a closer look at what is happening to your body.

During the last few weeks of pregnancy you were under unusual strain. There is a good chance that you felt uncomfortable physically and were worried about labor, delivery, the baby, and last minute details. Then labor began and you were probably performing the hardest kind of work that your body has ever been called upon to do. If the baby was born in the hospital, you then had a few days during which you were supposed to rest. But resting is not easy with the constant interruptions of a hospital routine. And you may have been so excited that relaxing and sleeping were difficult. Perhaps you had rooming-in, and you were partially responsible for your baby's care.

Eager as you probably were to return home, your arrival might not have turned out quite the way you had anticipated. Your trip home from the hospital, combined with your fatigue and discomfort, may have made you wonder how you would cope. Perhaps you were suddenly on the verge of tears when you expected to feel elated. The emotional ups and downs that many new mothers feel may be partly related to the abrupt hormonal changes that take place after birth. The relationship between hormonal imbalance and emotional instability is not clearly established. Moreover, some women may be more sensitive than others to such chemical changes in their bodies. Crying for no apparent reason during this period is not unusual. (See chapter 6 for a more detailed discussion of feelings of letdown and depression.)

You may also be wondering how long it will take your reproductive system to get back to normal now that the baby is born. A quick review of basic information might be helpful. During the first six weeks your uterus will be shrinking drastically, from two pounds to only three ounces. As it shrinks, it moves downward from its pregnant position to its original pelvic location and returns to its normal pear size.[1] As you probably know, breast-feeding helps the uterus return to normal more rapidly; contractions of the uterus (afterpains) that speed the process are often stimulated by nursing. Your cervix is contracting too. After expanding enough to allow your baby to pass into the vagina (birth canal), the cervix returns to its normal size in several weeks.

Your vagina may never return to precisely its pre-pregnant size, but by doing the Kegel exercise described in this chapter you will be able to tighten it considerably. It is normal for your genital area to feel slack during the first couple of weeks after giving birth. One of the amazing things about a woman's body is that it can expand so dramatically and then rapidly resume its usual size and shape—but it doesn't happen overnight.

Urination and Urinary Tract Infections

Because your entire pelvic floor (which includes the muscles and tissues surrounding your urethra, vagina, and rectum) has undergone a real trauma at the time of birth, it is natural that it will take time to recover. Simple bodily functions tend to take on huge significance during the first few days after giving birth. Urination, for example, may feel different to you for several weeks. This is not surprising when you consider that the baby was pressing on your bladder as she descended through your vagina. If a spinal anesthetic was used, it may have made your bladder less sensitive to how full it is and less able to empty itself completely.[2] Women who are unable to void within six or eight hours after delivery are usually catheterized to allow the urine to pass out of the body.

You will probably notice an increased need to urinate during the first week after delivery as the extra fluid you retained during pregnancy is being eliminated.[3] Many new mothers are extremely thirsty for a few days or notice that they perspire a lot.

Postpartum urinary tract infections are fairly common. Keep in mind the symptoms of such infections: fever, chills, discomfort upon urinating, inability to empty the bladder completely, frequent voiding in small amounts, and/or abdominal or back pain. While any one of these symptoms might signal a developing infection, it is unlikely that you will have all of them. Notify your doctor promptly if you think you have an infection, so it can be taken care of before a more serious problem develops.

Bowel Movements and Hemorrhoids

Giving birth is bound to have an effect on your intestines and rectum simply because of the pressure exerted on that area during delivery. In addition to sluggish bowels, you may develop swollen and tender lumps in your anus. These dilated veins, called hemorrhoids, tend to make bowel movements even more uncomfortable than they would otherwise be. It is not surprising that you may be reluctant to make a great effort to move your bowels since straining often causes hemorrhoids to become larger.

If the pain and swelling continue, inquire about using anesthetic creams or compresses, and take as many sitz baths as you can. Tucking hemorrhoids back in after a bowel movement seems to help too, but be sure not to use sharp fingernails. Drinking plenty of fluids and eating lots of fresh fruit, vegetables, and whole grain cereals will help keep your stools soft. A glass of prune juice followed by a cup of coffee in the morning may be helpful. If all your efforts prove ineffective, ask your doctor to recommend a mild laxative. If you are nursing, a stool softener (not a laxative) may help and will not affect your milk.

Stitches (Episiotomy)

Most doctors routinely make a short incision in the perineum in order to make more room for the baby's head at birth. The degree of discomfort you later feel in the area of your episiotomy is at least partly related to the skill with which the stitching was done and to the location and size of your incision.[4] It is a good idea to look at your episiotomy when the doctor or nurse is there so you can ask any questions you have about it. You may want to find out how you can tell by self-examination with a mirror whether the stitches are healing properly. When you get home, keep your genital area as dry and clean as possible by bathing frequently and changing sanitary napkins often. Some doctors give their patients alcohol swabs to use after urination and bowel movements which may prevent secondary infection and permit the stitches to heal rapidly. If you think the area is infected, notify your doctor right away to avoid the development of unnecessary scar tissue.[5]

The soreness that you feel results from the tissues in this area swelling and pulling against the stitches. This swelling usually reaches its peak about the third day after delivery and then begins to subside.[6] For some women the soreness lasts for two or three weeks; for others it is nearly gone within a week's time. If your pain is great and aspirin is not effective, talk to your doctor. Some doctors recommend local anesthetic sprays or salves to relieve the soreness, either instead of or in addition to oral medication.

It may help to know for future births that putting an ice pack on the area around your vagina as soon as possible after delivery will reduce the swelling and discomfort. As long as you aren't still anesthetized, ice is safe to use and, in the long run, is the most soothing treatment. You may even find an ice pack helpful after you return home. Another way to relieve soreness from stitches is to sit cross-legged on a hard surface or on a child's inflated plastic swimming ring.

Once the swelling has subsided, warm water and heat are effective in decreasing the soreness. Try using a regular sixty-watt light bulb twelve to fifteen inches away from the sore area while you are resting comfortably on a bed or sofa. Be sure not to use heat (or ice) if your genitals are numb from an anesthetic spray or cream since then you would not be able to feel the burning sensation that would warn you of too extreme a temperature. Warm showers, tub or sitz baths also help a lot. Use clear water; bath crystals and powders can be irritating to your genital area.

Finding time for heat treatments or bathing may seem impossible if you are alone and the baby's sleeping pattern is unpredictable. But it is very important that you begin *now* finding a way to care for yourself physically, even if you need help to do so. Arrange to have your husband or a friend look after the baby while you attend to your own personal needs.

The sooner you begin establishing such a pattern, the sooner you will regain your strength and feel like yourself again.

Vaginal Discharge

The bleeding that occurs following the delivery of the baby will continue until the place where the placenta was attached to your uterus has healed.[7] This vaginal discharge, called lochia, is likely to continue for the better part of a month or, for some women, up to six weeks. From a bright red color during the first week, it gradually turns paler and pinker, eventually losing its color. If at any time after the first week the bleeding increases markedly, be sure to notify your doctor.

You will need to use sanitary napkins for at least a week or two after you leave the hospital. The hospital-size napkins available at many drugstores are helpful at first. Sanitary napkins can be very awkward and irritating. If they really annoy you and press on your stitches, you may find that creams or alcohol compresses from the doctor or hospital are soothing. Self-adhesive sanitary napkins that adhere to your underpants may be less uncomfortable and are particularly suitable when the flow has decreased somewhat. Many doctors feel that tampons increase the likelihood of infection if used during the first several weeks, but you may want to inquire about using them again, particularly if your discharge continues beyond that time. Putting a small amount of lubricating jelly (such as K-Y, by Johnson and Johnson) on the end of the tampon may make insertion easier. Using tampons may help you feel that your vagina is returning to normal.

A continuing vaginal discharge with an unpleasant odor may indicate incomplete healing of the cervix or a vaginal infection and should be mentioned to your doctor so he can recommend treatment. Feminine hygiene deodorant sprays, nylon underwear, and panty hose tend to aggravate the problem; cotton pants, which "breathe" and stay drier, can help discourage persistent itching and infections.

The Kegel Exercise

The Kegel exercise, which involves tightening the muscles of your pelvic floor, will help relieve discomfort and improve the muscle tone and circulation in that area. All it requires is contracting the muscles of your anus, vagina, and urethra, one at a time, or all at once. Think of the muscles you use to hold in a bowel movement or to inhibit the flow of urine, then try to feel the different sensation of tightening your vagina. If you can remember to squeeze these muscles tightly about ten times in a row at least three times during the day, you will be well on your way toward getting your vagina and your pelvic floor muscles back into shape. One way to remind yourself is to make a point of trying to stop yourself midstream every time you urinate.

The Return of Menstruation

If you are not breast-feeding your baby, menstruation will probably begin again by the end of the second month after birth. Don't be alarmed if your first period seems peculiar. For some women it is heavy or prolonged; for others it is scanty or intermittent.[8] If you are breast-feeding, there is no sure way of predicting when menstruation will return—perhaps within a few months, or perhaps not until your baby is completely weaned. It seems to depend, in part, on how much you nurse and for how long. If you give your baby only breast milk, you are less likely to menstruate than if you feed her solid foods and supplementary bottles as well. Don't assume that you haven't ovulated simply because you haven't yet menstruated. It *is* necessary to take contraceptive precautions if you wish to avoid conceiving again. (See chapter 5 for a further discussion of contraception.)

Sore Breasts (Engorgement)

On the third or fourth day after delivery you may notice that you become engorged—your breasts suddenly become larger, firm, hot, and sore as your milk comes in. You may even have a headache and a brief low-grade fever.[9] Whereas breast-feeding mothers may expect to feel this soreness and discomfort, mothers who are bottle feeding often don't anticipate it. Even if you have been given a hormonal injection or pills to dry up your milk supply, your body may begin producing some milk anyway, and you can become engorged. If you don't plan to nurse, you should decrease fluids somewhat and avoid expressing milk from your breasts. Wearing a tight bra or pinning a towel or diaper tightly around your breasts twenty-four hours a day will help. In addition, applying an ice pack to the sore area and taking aspirin should bring relief. Within a few days the soreness should have subsided.

If you are not planning to nurse, you may feel upset if your milk comes in anyway. Even if you have carefully thought over your decision to bottle feed, the actual appearance of the milk may make you waver. You may feel suddenly confused and uncertain about what to do. If your breasts are sore and full, holding your baby close to them as you give her a bottle may seem "unfair" or "wrong." This response may be an emotional reaction to an unexpected experience rather than a reflection of your real feelings about breast- or bottle feeding. Such a reaction is understandable and shared by many women, and it will probably be only temporary. Still, you will need sympathetic support and a chance to express your feelings. If you actually are uncertain about which method to adopt, try to talk about it with someone who knows you well. Reading chapter 4, "The Breast-feeding Decision," may also help to clarify your feelings.

Some women experience a return of engorgement (to a lesser degree) during their first week home from the hospital. Don't be alarmed. Drinking a lot of fluids sometimes causes the milk glands to begin producing again, whether or not you are nursing. If you are not breast-feeding, continue to wear a bra or diaper pinned tightly around you, and the engorgement will soon subside.

If you are breast-feeding, try putting warm washcloths on your breasts or letting your baby nurse briefly, even if it is between feedings. Expressing milk manually may also help relieve the pressure. If your breasts feel hard and expressing milk is painful, a warm shower sometimes starts the milk flowing. Try to protect your tender nipples from the direct spray. Remember as you relieve the pressure, however, that the more milk you express, the more your body will produce. So don't express too much during the days before your baby's appetite has grown. Engorgement usually diminishes as your body begins to produce only as much milk as your baby needs. If you continue to have problems you can use alternate massage: when the baby is nursing at one breast, massage the other breast toward the nipple. (For a description of other causes of breast soreness, see chapter 4.)

Your Shape and Appetite

If you were eagerly anticipating a flat stomach after delivery, the discovery that you haven't yet returned to your pre-pregnant size may disappoint you. This fact is not surprising, however, since the average woman loses only thirteen and a half pounds at the time of delivery and an additional three or four pounds during the following two weeks.[10]

You may be especially discouraged if you find that you don't fit into anything but your old maternity clothes. If possible, consider making, borrowing, or buying something special to wear at this time. A colorful dress or bathrobe might be a real morale booster. Or maybe a new top to wear with a pair of loose-fitting jeans, elasticized pants, or a wraparound skirt would make you feel comfortable. If you are nursing, don't forget to choose something you can feed the baby in easily. If you buy ahead, remember that your bust size is likely to be larger during the months you nurse.

Eager as you may be to lose weight and return to your former size and shape, you may find yourself extremely hungry and without the time or energy to prepare enticing, well-balanced meals. The sensible thing, of course, is to eat only nutritious foods. But there are times when these seem too exhausting to prepare or don't seem satisfying. You may find yourself tempted to snack a lot, particularly if you are feeling anxious or depressed. Try to keep healthful snacks around. Such things as slices of cheese, hard-boiled eggs, yogurt, carrot and celery sticks, cold sliced meat, vitamin-enriched cold cereals (or familia or granola), fresh fruit, and fruit juices may just hit the spot if they are easy to locate. Although not all of these foods are low in calories, eaten in reasonable quantities

they should help keep your energy high without causing unnecessary weight gain. If they are ready when you are hungry,
your mind may not dwell on less nutritious and more fattening
foods. If you don't get upset about the way you look and are
sensible about your intake of food, the chances are good that
your weight will begin to take care of itself. If it continues to
bother you, ask your doctor for advice. *Don't resort to diet pills.*
At this time of fatigue, tension, and hormonal change, they
could have disastrous effects.

Exercise and Exertion

For the first week after delivery make a special effort not to
exert yourself unduly. To save energy, plan your activities so
that once you are upstairs you remain there for a while.
There's no reason why you shouldn't go for a short walk once
you feel up to it. The fresh air will feel good and the change
of scene may lift your spirits. Driving a car and running short
errands are also fine once you feel comfortable again. Since
traveling any great distance can be very exhausting, try not to
plan any long trips until the baby is close to a month old.[11]
Consider your physical condition carefully before you begin
any strenuous exercise program. Exercise can revitalize you,
but you do not want to exhaust your physical resources.

Postpartum Checkup

Your doctor will want to see you again several weeks after
you have given birth. If you are anxious during the pelvic exam,
remember to breathe deeply and try to relax. Many women
find such exams less uncomfortable after childbirth than they
were before. This is an excellent time to ask your doctor anything that bothers you about how back-to-normal you really
are and to talk about contraception. If you have already had
intercourse and experienced any problems, mention them and
ask for helpful suggestions. If your doctor is supportive of
breast-feeding and you have any questions, feel free to ask for
help. Although it may seem aggressive to you to raise so many
issues, it is important to get your fears and uncertainties out
in the open so they don't get distorted and grow in your mind.

Many women find it helpful to write down their questions, so they won't be intimidated by a doctor who appears to be in a hurry. While he may not be able to give you all the emotional support you feel you need, your doctor should be able to clarify many of the things that are troubling you.

If questions arise after your checkup, call and ask the nurse about them, or ask to speak with the doctor directly if you prefer. If your doctor really isn't helpful and responsive, and you are continuing to have problems, you may want to change to another one. It is worth the time, effort, and money involved if you are not getting satisfactory care and assistance. All of this is emphasized not so much because you are apt to have problems as because if you do experience difficulties, it is crucial to deal with them as soon as possible. You are under too many other pressures to let continued discomfort add to your tension.

Coming to Terms with Your Body

Some women feel very good after their postpartum checkup. They are happy to see their doctor, pleased to know they are recovering well, and feel they have communicated their worries and received the reassurance they were looking for. For other women the postpartum checkup is accompanied by a letdown or disappointed feeling. For some women more than others there is a necessary process of coming to terms with their bodies after childbirth, either physically or emotionally. In some cases this problem comes into focus at the time of the checkup.

Some women, for example, feel uneasy about physical changes that may or may not disappear with time. It can take a while to adjust to stretch marks, varicose veins, hemorrhoids, changes in your breasts, hair falling out, or a flabby stomach. Some women are also surprised by how long genital soreness continues. Perhaps you have already tried having intercourse and experienced problems. You may be reluctant to look at your genital area with a mirror or have irrational fears that making love will never be as satisfying for you as it once was. Discovering these changes and discomforts and being unsure of how to interpret them can be upsetting.

Even if your feelings are triggered by specific changes in your body, the problem may not be adjusting to the changes so much as dealing with the feelings they create. You may sense a certain "loss of innocence" in your body and feel that you have passed from girlhood to motherhood with no way back. The change lies partly in your body, partly in the experience you have been through. Childbirth is one aspect of your sexuality: the experience of bodies slipping in and out of each other, the tremendous buildup and release of tension, the joy and possibly the sadness or the pain you might have felt. Perhaps you are still sorting out the impact that participating in birth has had on you. How does it fit together with day-to-day life? How can it "end" in a routine checkup?

You may have been keeping your feelings in the back of your mind, not sure how to sort them out, hoping that with this last reunion with your doctor you would have gone full circle, and your doubts would be resolved, your body back to its former condition. The focus is exclusively on you at this appointment —perhaps for the first time since the birth. You may suddenly be acutely aware that at least some of the changes—both physical and emotional—are here to stay. At times it is difficult to accept things that are irreversible and be confident that they will be the basis of a new and deeper understanding of yourself and possibly even a greater satisfaction with yourself physically.

The more you clarify your vague fears about your physical well-being and get them out into the open, the more likely you are to find the reassurance you need. Talking your feelings over with your husband will probably help a lot and make you both feel closer. If you take the time to talk about this experience that means so much to both of you, you will have a common basis for continuing to understand the feelings you have rather than discounting them as irrelevant or unpleasant.

TACKLING DAY-TO-DAY PROBLEMS TOGETHER

Taking care of your physical needs during this period and accepting the wide range of feelings that you both have will help you get on your feet as parents. But what about the day-to-day tasks involved in simply keeping a household functioning? How are these to be managed under such circumstances, particularly when one or both of you are feeling so exhausted? Adding a baby to a household increases the total workload many times over. It's not just a simple matter of feeding, changing, and keeping the baby and related paraphernalia clean. Over and above these tasks is the time spent comforting a crying baby, sometimes at the most inconvenient moments of the day or night. A couple can no longer count on an evening of relaxation or even a quiet dinner together. Both of you may find it hard to predict when you will have any time to yourselves. The resulting physical, emotional, and mental fatigue that you are apt to feel is obviously going to affect your ability to cope with day-to-day tasks.

Combating Fatigue

For the first couple of weeks it is important that new mothers take at least one nap each day. Napping when the baby sleeps is one way of approaching the problem, but if the baby doesn't sleep much during the day, someone else should relieve the mother so she can sleep. When babies do take long naps, their mothers are often tempted to use that time to catch up on housework. Not resting enough at the beginning, however, may lead to sudden exhaustion later. Some women have enough energy to get through the first few weeks without any serious stress or strain. Their lack of sleep eventually catches up with them though, and by then the baby may be sleeping less and needing more attention. It may be harder then to regain the strength needed to get through a day without collapsing.

Visits and phone calls are important and exciting in the early weeks, but you should both feel free to explain to friends and relatives that you will call them when you feel ready for company. Another solution is simply to smother the telephone with a pillow or take it off the hook during the mother's rest period or bath time if she is home alone.

New parents often don't realize how tired they are. Either

of you may at times feel tense and irritable and find it hard to relax. Rather than becoming annoyed when this happens, the two of you can help each other by remembering that tension and irritability are signs of overexertion. Try to get more rest. If tension continues to mount, and unwinding becomes impossible, feel free to call the doctor. Some will prescribe a mild tranquilizer on a short term basis.

Getting Down to Basics

One way to overcome fatigue is to reduce the number of household tasks to only those you view as really important. Some couples find that it helps to agree first on a list of essentials and then talk over what each person feels up to doing. Agreeing on the tasks that really must be done will help both of you feel less guilty about not doing others. Relaxing is just as important as vacuuming, if not more so, so don't let a little household dirt stand in the way of getting some rest. Limiting your work to the bare essentials and sharing those tasks in a reasonable way may leave you enough time and energy to be in touch with each other and to sense each other's needs and feelings. In the long run, your sensitivity to each other will be a major factor in keeping alive your sense of humor as you figure out the best way to get the work done.

One very important decision you can make is to accept all the help you can get. If you post your list of essentials in a prominent place, or bring it out for a frank discussion with friends or relatives, they will probably not hesitate to fill in where they are really needed. The jobs may not be glamorous, but the volunteers will know for sure that they are helping in the most important ways. Even if they don't always do things the way you would, let them do the best they can. The situation is only temporary; you can always do things your way in a few weeks, if that is important to you. If you happen to have relatives or acquaintances who insist on helping but rub one or both of you the wrong way in times of stress, give them jobs that minimize your actual contact. Perhaps they could make you a batch of spaghetti or run a few errands for your family.

THE SPECIAL CASE OF A CESAREAN SECTION

In many ways convalescing from a Cesarean section is similar to recovering from a vaginal delivery. Be sure to read the preceding pages that are relevant in this regard. There are important differences, however; after all, C-sections are considered major abdominal surgery.

The percentage of Cesarean sections has increased markedly in recent years as the operation has become so much safer. Some doctors now estimate that C-sections make up nearly one-tenth of all deliveries; others quote a slightly lower figure. Of all the C-sections performed, about fifty percent are repeats; the other half are done under very specific kinds of obstetrical situations involving the health and safety of either mother or child, or both.[12]

Why a C-Section?

Cesarean sections are usually unexpected the first time they occur. The progress of labor frequently determines the doctor's decision to operate. Although it can be very upsetting to go through many hours of difficult labor and then give birth by Cesarean section, there is usually no way to shortcut this process. This "trial labor" or test of labor is often the only way the doctor can determine whether a vaginal delivery will be possible. Understandably, couples often feel disappointed when such a decision is made. On the other hand, many feel intensely relieved that the long hours of labor are at last over and their baby is finally born.

There are many reasons for performing a Cesarean section. In some cases the baby turns out to be too large for the mother's pelvic structure. This situation is often coupled with an unfavorable position of the baby (perhaps either transverse or breech) or with uterine contractions that prove unable to cause the cervix to dilate completely. Sometimes bleeding complications or maternal health hazards are present. If at any time the baby's heartbeat (monitored externally or internally) indicates that she is not getting enough oxygen, perhaps because of a twisted umbilical cord, a C-section will be performed to insure a quick and safe delivery.[13] Be sure to ask your doctor for the details of your particular situation. Understanding the reasons behind the decision to operate will help you accept your feelings about it.

The operation itself takes less than an hour. If a regional anesthetic is used, you can remain awake throughout, and then see your baby immediately following delivery. If a general anesthetic is used, it will be a few hours before you will be alert enough to see the baby. Sometimes C-section newborns are placed under observation for several hours. If this occurs, it is probably a routine precaution, but you should ask for reassurance from your doctor if you are worried about your baby.

Both of you will probably be eager to see what your baby is like. The father can probably take a look as the baby is wheeled out of the operating room. As the baby's mother, you should feel free to ask a nurse to bring your new child into your room as soon as you feel up to it. If there is any problem with this, try to contact your doctor. Although you may find it hard to believe that your baby is really born if you haven't been as involved as you expected in the birth, holding her may help the reality sink in and lift your spirits. The more time you spend with your newborn, the sooner you will believe that you are now a mother and this is indeed your baby.

Your Feelings Following a C-Section

Your feelings following a C-section will depend in part on the circumstances of your operation. If surgery came as a total shock to you, perhaps after many hours of tiring labor, you may feel anxious or upset about what happened. Although glad that it is finally over, you may feel disappointed or even cheated that you weren't able to give birth in the usual way. Especially if the two of you had spent weeks attending childbirth preparation classes, you may be very disappointed that both of you couldn't participate as fully in your baby's birth as you had hoped. Fathers, too, may feel isolated and let down at not being able to be with their wives and watch the delivery.

Although it can be very difficult to express your disappointment, sharing your feelings with each other will help. Hospital staff and visitors will probably try to focus on the joyful aspects of the situation and ignore the negative feelings that may be just as real. You may be wondering "Why me?" and ask yourself whether the operation was really necessary. Talking to your doctor about what happened and why will probably help you to accept the fact that your baby was born in the safest way possible.

If you knew in advance that you would be having a C-section, you may have been better prepared emotionally for the experience. Understanding the reasons for performing the operation and not having to go through the trial labor can make the next few days a little bit easier. Still, you may feel disappointed, especially when you see women who have just had vaginal deliveries get up and move around sooner and more easily than you can. Whatever your feelings, don't try to hide them. By sharing your reactions with each other, close friends, and your doctor, you will be able to accept those feelings sooner, and you'll be ready to move on to the challenges ahead.

Physical Problems Related to Cesarean Deliveries

General discomfort. You will have a certain amount of abdominal pain and discomfort for the first two or three days. You may also feel pain in your shoulders that is caused by blood and air collecting under your diaphragm and irritating it.[14] Sedatives are available if you need them, but you should feel markedly better on each successive day.

Diet. C-section mothers usually receive intravenous fluids from the time of the operation until some time the next day. A liquid diet follows the i.v., in most cases, for about another day. Then comes a soft diet, including only foods that can be easily digested. The following day the dietary restrictions are usually lifted, and meals begin to include roughage, meats, etc. When you get home, you should make a special effort to eat balanced meals with plenty of protein. Good nutrition and plenty of rest are important for a full and speedy recovery.

Urination. The catheter that was inserted into your bladder prior to surgery may remain in place for a day or two after delivery. Once you are able to get out of bed and go to the bathroom more or less unassisted, it will be removed. Since the catheter may increase your chances of getting a urinary tract infection and/or urethral irritation, keep in mind the symptoms of such problems (mentioned earlier in this chapter) so you can alert the doctor if they develop.

Bowel movements. Following your operation you will probably find that your bowels are very sluggish. The operation itself, plus your postoperative limited diet and inactivity, are all contributing factors. Since straining in an effort to have a bowel movement is nearly impossible after a C-section, it is important to do everything you can to keep your stools soft. Drink plenty of fluids, eat roughage and whole grain cereals as soon as you are able, and inquire about taking a stool softener if you think it would help.

Gas and gas pains. About the third day after the operation, your intestines will begin to function again, and you will probably feel sharp gas pains. However uncomfortable these pains are for you, your doctor will view them as a good sign. The fact that gas is being moved down the intestinal tract means that there is no infection causing intestinal difficulties.[15] Getting up and moving around will help get your system going again. Rolling from side to side in your bed and changing positions will also help your body get rid of the gas. Sleeping on your stomach sometimes helps, too, even though getting into that position may hurt. Also, try placing the baby on your upper abdomen when she is brought to you for feedings. If you are nursing, try putting her on a pillow on your stomach. In both cases the baby's weight will tend to push the gas down and bring you relief.

Incision. The dressing covering a C-section incision is usually removed about a day after the operation. Don't be alarmed if your abdomen hurts more after the bandage is removed; this may result simply because the bandage no longer acts as a support. You may notice that your incision oozes a bit. Worrying about disrupting your stitches is unnecessary since this almost never happens. Toward the end of your hospital stay, they will be removed unless they are the kind that are automatically absorbed.

You will be given injections and/or pills to ease the pain and discomfort. Although you should certainly ask for medication when you feel you need it, you may want to try to get along with as little as possible since many kinds of pain medications tend to aggravate gas and constipation problems. Because pressure on your incision increases your discomfort, you may want to avoid using a sanitary belt. At first you can pin the hospital-size sanitary napkins to your underpants; once the discharge has diminished somewhat, you may want to switch to the self-adhesive kind or consider using tampons.

Complications. If at any time you feel feverish, be sure to notify your doctor. While not common, postoperative complications can and do occur. Internal infections sometimes develop, as do infections in the incision itself. Excessive vaginal bleeding also signals the need for medical attention. This may prolong your stay in the hospital, but since most complications are effectively treated with antibiotics, you will soon be ready to go home. Infections do slow up a woman's recovery, however, so be certain that you have adequate help once you return home.

Answers to Other Questions You May Have

Breast-feeding after a C-section. There is no reason why you shouldn't nurse your baby if you want to. See chapter 4 for help with breast-feeding.

Resuming sex. You are apt to experience fewer discomforts on resuming sex than women who have had a vaginal delivery. Ask your doctor if there are any special precautions he would suggest, and once you are ready to resume intercourse, plan to use positions where there is the least amount of pressure directly on your incision.

Conception and contraception. Most doctors feel it is safe to get pregnant again three months after a C-section delivery. But do check with your doctor if you want to conceive again in those first few months. If the thought of enduring a future Cesarean frightens you, keep in mind that the experience is likely to be far less traumatic the second time around. Knowing what to expect and not having to go through the trial labor can help considerably. The reasoning behind the saying "once a C-section, always a C-section" is that most doctors are reluctant to risk rupturing the original scar on the uterus during labor, however slight the chance. Remember that even if you are nursing, you must use contraceptive measures to avoid possible pregnancy. (See "Re-evaluating Your Method of Birth Control," chapter 5.)

Further restrictions on activities. The restrictions placed on you as a C-section mother are somewhat different from those placed on other new mothers. First of all, you are likely to remain in the hospital for several days longer than most women who have vaginal deliveries—perhaps as many as seven or eight days. Once home again, you will probably be advised either to eliminate or drastically reduce climbing stairs for the next two weeks. It is important that you not lift anything heavier than your baby during the month following the operation. (This becomes more of a problem after a second baby is born, since you won't be able to lift your first child.) Postoperative restrictions vary with different doctors and different women. Since your doctor is the only person who fully understands your medical circumstances, be sure to discuss restrictions with him.

Feeling Let Down and Exhausted Is Normal

All new mothers feel tired and let down at some point or other. You may possess these feelings to a stronger degree, however, particularly as you see other women come and go following vaginal deliveries. In addition to a longer hospital stay, you must cope with the strain and bodily trauma of major surgery. It may not seem at all fair, and you may wonder where you are going to find the strength to get through the next couple of weeks.

The more tired you get, the more likely you are to feel

discouraged and depressed. It makes sense to limit your activities until your strength begins to return; doing too much too soon is apt to make you feel you can't cope. Try not to become impatient with feelings of fatigue and physical weakness, and don't let your inability to accomplish much get you down. The more you rest now, the sooner you'll recover. Do your best to take care of yourself, and accept all offers of help that come your way. Then, if you are still feeling really low, talk to your doctor. Medication is available for women who need it, so don't be embarrassed or ashamed to ask for it.

Eager as you will be to let your friends and relatives see your baby, restricting visitors is another necessity. For the first two weeks it is important to do little else than convalesce and take care of the essentials of baby care. Do not let yourself feel guilty about postponing visits, even with close relatives. Your recovery is the most important thing right now. It may seem as though it takes forever, but by the time five or six weeks have elapsed, you will be feeling much stronger and healthier —if you take it easy right from the beginning.

A new group has been formed to help C-section parents. Cesarean Sections, Education and Concern (C/SEC) is a non-profit organization that strives to educate and support couples who give birth by Cesarean section. In order to make the experience as meaningful and rewarding as possible, C/SEC is trying to establish family centered Cesarean maternity care as well as to help childbirth educators, doctors, nurses, and the Cesarean couples themselves better understand the physical and emotional components of Cesarean deliveries. Significant progress has already been made toward attaining these goals in the Boston area where C/SEC originated. For information regarding membership and the group's newsletter, write to Nancy Cohen, Co-founder, 140 Valley Rd., Needham, Mass. 02192.

RECOMMENDED READING

Boston Children's Medical Center. *Pregnancy, Birth and the Newborn Baby.* New York: Delacorte, Seymour Lawrence, 1971, 1972.

This book is an attempt on the part of the Boston Children's Medical Center to offer parents a broad view of childbearing. The center consulted with many specialists in creating the book, which combines the insights of anthropology, sociology, animal behavior, psychology, and medicine. It presents information on pregnancy, birth and its impact on parents and the newborn baby. A separate part of the book deals with special problems relating to conception and pregnancy and a discussion of genetics. Each part covers basics and includes information that is often not emphasized in other sources, such as diseases and conditions that complicate pregnancy, complications of labor and delivery, a detailed description of the checkup a newborn is given in the hospital, and a list of diseases and disorders of newborns. The book has a broad scope which could be nicely supplemented by more detailed guides to each aspect of childbearing. It is expensive but brings together a lot of information that parents or parents-to-be might have difficulty finding. It has a thought-provoking approach and is worth looking at.

Boston Women's Health Book Collective. *Our Bodies, Ourselves.* New York: Simon and Schuster, 1971, 1973.

This book was written by a group of Boston women who feel that a woman's understanding of her body can give her a deeper sense of herself and more control over her life. The book includes material on physical, emotional, and sexual aspects of women's lives and relationships: women's changing sense of self, the anatomy and physiology of reproduction and sexuality, sexuality in relationships, nutrition, exercise, rape and self-defense, venereal disease, birth control, abortion, deciding whether to have children, childbearing, and menopause. The book stresses the inadequacy of the current health care system and shows the effect of prevailing social attitudes on how women feel about their bodies and themselves. It gives many concrete suggestions for change. The section on childbearing includes a discussion of the postpartum time—both physical and psychological aspects—and emphasizes ways of giving women and families more support to minimize the strain they are under. The book is an important source of information and can provide a new mother with a broader sense of herself in relation to others at a time when she may feel very isolated and especially in need of this perspective.

2

Taking Care of Your Baby

ALL NEW PARENTS FEEL UNEASY

The Sudden Shock of Responsibility

It may not really hit you until you bring the baby home from the hospital that now there is no turning back, no chance of having the baby whisked away and cared for by experts. This sudden realization that the baby is now yours, twenty-four hours a day, and that you must take care of her can be overwhelming. Even with family and friends around to share the physical work and give you moral support as you muddle through the first days as a family, nothing takes away the feeling of awe that ultimately you are the parents of this child, day and night, whether you feel up to it or not, whether you know how to be or not. This irreversible responsibility is different from any other you have undertaken. As excited as you probably are to be on your own, it is perfectly understandable that you may feel uneasy about your ability to handle the situation.

Parenting Is a New Skill

Caring for a tiny baby involves learning many new skills. There is nothing instinctive about diapering or bathing a newborn. Even feeling comfortable when holding a baby is something that you learn with time and experience. More difficult still is the problem of knowing what to do when a newborn cries; it is hard to sense what your baby is feeling and know how to comfort her when feeding and holding don't seem adequate. You may also find that the routine of feeding your baby—whether by bottle or breast—takes a while to establish comfortably, and doesn't necessarily come naturally. You are both apt to feel awkward for a while in all these new situations. But feeling awkward in no way means you are inadequate. It simply means you haven't been parents long enough to feel comfortable one hundred percent of the time.

Even parents who have done a great deal of baby-sitting in the past, or who have friends with young children, find caring for their own child's needs to be quite a different sort of challenge. Fortunately, the necessary skills do develop as the days pass. Comparing notes with friends who recently have had babies can be very helpful as long as you remember how different each newborn is. Often one of you will hit upon a new approach that solves a problem that had baffled the other. Sharing problems and ideas with others will help keep you from feeling so alone at the beginning.

Newborns Often Look Strange
Either one of you may have feelings about your baby that you hadn't anticipated. Although to some parents a newborn actually looks strikingly beautiful from the moment of birth, your baby may look very different than you had imagined and may not even be the sex you had been hoping for. She may even strike you as disappointingly unattractive. The newborn baby's genitals and breasts may be swollen; girl babies sometimes have a slight flow from the vagina, either pink or white in color. Your baby's umbilical cord may look peculiar. If redness or discharge develops around her navel, you should notify the doctor since these may be signs of infection; otherwise it is best to leave it alone. Simply keep the cord dry until it falls off in one to three weeks; baths can wait. If forceps have been used during the delivery, the baby's head may be somewhat bruised and temporarily misshapen. A newborn's ears and nose are sometimes flattened and pushed off to one side. Red spots and rashes of various sorts are common, especially on the face. Scaly skin and flaky scalp are often noticeable, and some babies are born with fine hair covering much of their bodies. Occasionally a newborn's long fingernails will scratch her own tender skin, marring still further her already strange appearance.

None of these things should be cause for alarm. With time your baby will appear quite normal and acceptable to you, and you will forget that she once looked so peculiar. Be sure to ask your baby's doctor about anything that bothers you, but rest assured that within several weeks, your baby's appearance will improve.

Love at First Sight?

Contrary to popular myth, many new mothers and fathers find that love for their baby is not instantaneous. Love for an infant usually develops gradually, and is often not felt strongly until the baby begins to show pleasure in response to the care and attention you give her. When your baby begins to smile at you and clearly enjoys your presence, you may feel a stronger relationship developing. Sometimes it takes longer for a father to develop close feelings for his baby if he is away all day. There is no need to feel guilty or disappointed if you find that the process takes longer than you expected. Particularly if you were hoping for a child of the other sex, it is natural that it will take a while for you to feel really comfortable with the one you actually got.

Babies as a Reflection on Their Parents

The notion that relaxed parents have relaxed babies is destructive and misleading. Naturally it is helpful to take the awkwardness and difficulty of the first weeks in your stride as much as possible. But even if you are extremely relaxed, your baby might still be uncomfortable or irritable because of inborn physical and temperamental characteristics over which you have no control. Beyond their physical dissimilarities, more is now known about differences in newborn babies' temperaments. Your baby picks up many signals from the way you touch and relate to her, but she has a unique way of reacting as well. Feeling that your baby's fussiness and tenseness are your fault will only make you more tense, and may actually prevent you from handling the situation calmly and objectively. For many parents and babies, the process of relaxing and accepting one another takes a while. But seeing your baby as a reflection on you makes the process take longer and obscures the fact that she is a person with her own problems and pleasures, who will be a challenge for you to get to know and love.

Newborns Seem So Vulnerable

Even if your baby has been examined and declared healthy, she probably seems incredibly small and vulnerable to you. This is bound to make you feel uneasy—especially during the first few weeks, when it is natural for you to worry about causing discomfort or even injury to your baby. Diaper pins seem clumsy and nail scissors don't seem to be the right size for tiny fingernails. (Try clipping nails when the baby is asleep.) Bathing a wriggly, slippery baby can also be nerve-wracking. To minimize your uneasiness, try rolling up a towel for a pillow and then lay the baby down in only an inch or two of water in a plastic tub. Another possibility is to take the baby into a shallow lukewarm bath with you. This works out best if there are two adults around since you may need help getting out of the tub together.

Knowing that no serious accidents are likely to occur doesn't necessarily keep you from worrying. The fact is, though, that babies are a lot tougher than they first appear. They are well able to withstand the awkward handling they often receive from their parents during those first few weeks. Newborns are equipped with all the abilities they need to function—breathing, sucking, swallowing, and getting rid of wastes. They can look around, hear, taste, feel, turn their heads, and cry for help right from the beginning.[1] As you get used to having this tiny baby around, she will not seem quite so frail or small.

Taking the Baby Outdoors

You may wonder when you can take your baby outside. In pleasant weather there's nothing wrong with taking her out as soon as you feel up to it yourself. Going for a walk can be a refreshing activity for all of you. If you plan to be away for more than a short time, however, keep in mind that newborns are more sensitive to temperature than you and may need more protection, especially from heat. You may want to stay away from large crowds at first if you are worried about coughers and sneezers. If you meet neighbors with peculiar notions about keeping babies indoors until they can walk and talk, don't let them alarm or upset you. You may at times get the impression that everyone in the world feels like an expert on bringing up your baby. Thank them for the advice and ignore it if you wish.

The First Illness

The first time your baby gets sick, you are apt to become quite worried, and may even feel guilty about having exposed the baby to whatever germs she has caught. Although colds are usually mild in infants, the first one may seem really serious to you since you don't know what to expect. Putting a cold-mist humidifier in the baby's room usually helps; at least you'll know she is breathing more easily.

Don't be reluctant to call the doctor if you notice unusual symptoms, particularly a fever. Remember that infants' bowel movements may vary a lot in smell, color, and consistency. Be sure to report any that are either bloody or very watery, and ask your own doctor for guidelines on other changes in stools that might be of concern. Repeated vomiting, unusual crying, listlessness, inability to sleep, loss of appetite, and rashes are some of the symptoms that might indicate illness.[2] Doctors usually want to know when a tiny baby gets sick, even if it turns out to be only a slight cold. Be sure to take the baby's temperature *before* calling the doctor, and jot down the symptoms you have noticed so you won't forget to mention them. If possible both parents should have the experience of calling the doctor and accompanying the baby to the doctor's office, so that both of you can become acquainted with his approach and routine.

Hopefully the baby's doctor and nurse will be as supportive of you as they are skilled in diagnosing and treating illnesses. New parents need reassurance as well as information in order to gain confidence. Be sure you understand exactly what the doctor or nurse is explaining and recommending, and write it down. Although their routines will eventually make sense to you, until they do you will probably feel anxious and uncertain. You don't want to be fussy and overprotective, but it seems impossible to be casual. An infant's illness can be as hard on the parents themselves as it is on the baby!

It's Hard to Know for Sure

As the days pass, one frustrating thing you discover is that there really aren't definitive answers to many of the questions that arise. You want to be sure you are doing what's best for the baby, but many of the situations that come up leave you feeling confused. Why does your baby cry so much? After feeding and changing, you put her down for a nap, but she continues to be fussy and fretful. Should you pick her up again or just let her cry for a while, waiting to see whether she will fall asleep soon? You read that feelings of basic trust and security are fostered at this time. If you let your baby cry, what effect will it have? What will it do to the feelings she is developing about you and the world? Can a baby be lonely at the age of a month or two? Can you spoil an infant with too much handling? What is colic, anyway, and what should parents do for a colicky baby? Will the baby suffer if the mother decides to stop breast-feeding sooner than originally planned? Is it true that relaxed parents have calm and contented babies? What are you doing wrong?

Even if you consult your child care books faithfully, listen to the advice of parents and friends, and call the baby's doctor or nurse, you aren't likely to get clear answers to such questions; they are part of the atmosphere of uncertainty that you are living in as parents. You have to make the best decisions you can under these circumstances. The more you expect to have complete control, the harder it is to accept the uncertainty you hadn't anticipated. Chances are you will become more relaxed as you begin to realize how unique the combination of you and your baby is. More likely than not your own sense of what is appropriate will be as good or better than the advice of people who know your baby less intimately than you do. If you concentrate on getting to know your baby rather than having the right answers, you'll relax more and enjoy being parents. It's a real challenge to gather the conflicting advice, take a good look at the situation yourselves, and then make your own decision.

WHAT ARE NEWBORNS LIKE?

Babies Have Different Temperaments

New parents who come into close contact with tiny infants other than their own soon discover that no two babies are alike. One baby sucks vigorously, finishing a meal in five or ten minutes, while another has a leisurely feeding and is easily distracted by nearby noises and lights. Some babies sleep a lot, awakening at regular intervals to drink fairly predictable amounts of milk. Others are far less regular, sleeping and eating in what seems to be a haphazard fashion. Some babies cry frequently and with a surprising intensity; others barely whimper even when a feeding is long overdue. The explanation for these differences in style lies in each baby's temperament.

From birth infants have unique ways of responding to hunger, noise, cold, wetness, sleep, new experiences—everything that happens in their lives. Even if handled very similarly by the adults who care for them, children react and cope differently. Parents with two or more children can attest to this fact. All their best techniques for soothing the first child, for example, may turn out to be ineffective with the second. As you get to know your baby, you will be able to watch her style and personality unfold. And you will discover that her characteristic way of responding affects you, just as your way of handling her influences her growth and development. All three of you are contributing to the relationship that gradually emerges. Understanding this can help you develop ways of interacting with your child that you feel good about and that take into account her uniqueness as a person.

Unfortunately, individual differences among babies are often overlooked in books on baby care. Although they may give lip service to individuality, such books often fail to describe the wide range of normal behavior and are in fact filled with generalizations about "typical" infants. You wonder, then, what you are doing that makes your baby act differently from those you read about or other babies you see.

There are a number of ways in which infants differ in temperament. An awareness of these will help you understand your child better and make your expectations more appropriate. You may also find that you become more sensitive to other children's temperaments and more accepting of the problems and pleasures other parents are experiencing. The following list of ways in which infants differ is included to give you a starting point for thinking about your baby. It is based on the one used by Drs. Chess, Birch, and Thomas in their New York Longitudinal Study of Child Development.[3]

Whether or not you can figure out exactly what your baby's responses are in each category, reading this list will give you some insight into the range of temperamental responses that exists. And you may understand better why your baby reacts or behaves in certain ways. Since not all aspects of temperament emerge at birth, it may be helpful to look at the list again in several weeks or months.

1. Activity Level: Does your baby move around a lot, or does she remain surprisingly still for long periods of time? How much twisting and turning does she do while you put on a diaper or clothes? Does she often squirm out from under the covers and kick vigorously as she lies on a blanket or sits in an infant seat?

2. Regularity: Is your baby predictable with respect to eating, sleeping, and bowel movements? Do you usually know when she will want to eat and how hungry she will be? Or is she quite unscheduled and erratic?

3. Approach or Withdrawal: How does your baby usually react the first time she encounters new people, new foods, and new situations (the first bath, first stroller ride, a new face)? Does she seem pleased with the new event, or does she shy away and withdraw, perhaps fussing or even screaming?

4. Adaptability to Change in Routine: Babies' routines change a lot as they grow and develop and as the needs of their parents change. How easily does your baby adjust to a change? Does she usually adapt readily to new people, new situations, and new schedules, or does it often take many exposures for your baby to feel comfortable with the new object or experience? Do you find yourselves adapting your

lives to your baby's schedule, or can you expect your baby to adjust to a schedule that is convenient for you without too much difficulty?

5. Level of Sensory Threshold: Does your infant startle easily at loud noises? Become annoyed by bright lights? Seem bothered by rough clothes, or by being hot or cold, wet or dry? Does pain (such as a bump or scratch) bring a howl of discomfort or barely a whimper?

6. Positive or Negative Mood: Is your child generally friendly and contented, or frequently fussy and dissatisfied, even after a nap and a feeding? Does she cry a lot upon awakening, when put down after being held, when going to sleep?

7. Intensity of Response: Does your baby cry loudly and intensely, or fairly quietly in comparison to others you've heard? How does she express happy feelings—with a mild smile, vigorous chortling, gurgling or kicking? Does she seem to have a lot of energy to put into eating, fussing, and generally moving about?

8. Distractibility: How easy is it to draw your child's attention away from what she is doing? If you are feeding your baby, will she keep on sucking no matter what noises occur nearby? If she is crying, can she be easily distracted with a toy or a change of position?

9. Persistence and Attention Span: How long will your infant stick with an activity, even if she finds it difficult, or is interrupted? The persistent child keeps trying to reach a toy that is out of reach; the nonpersistent one tries only a few times. The persistent child keeps fighting experiences she dislikes, like being washed, whereas the nonpersistent child gives in very quickly.

Learning more about your particular child's way of behaving and reacting will suggest to you new ways of working with her temperament instead of against it. If, for example, your baby withdraws from new experiences, you may want to introduce them gradually. Rather than giving yourself either the credit or blame for having such a child, recognize that she was born that way and needs to be handled with understanding. Your job is to help your baby become less uneasy with new experiences and learn to adapt to changing circumstances gradually. You should not expect instant success, nor should you feel apologetic if your child protests or becomes quiet and withdrawn. You'll know what is fair to expect because you understand what your child is like.

One of the problems with most performance charts (descriptions of when most babies learn new skills) is that they do not take temperament into account. An active and persistent baby might roll over at two months, for example, but a perfectly normal less active, less persistent child might not roll over until several months later. The quiet child, in the meantime, might be focusing attention on sounds, patterns, or colors. It really makes sense to discover what is intriguing to your child, rather than worrying about what she isn't showing interest in doing. Only extreme deviations from the norms described in books are worth worrying about and should be mentioned to your baby's doctor.

Recognizing your baby's strengths and difficulties will help you view your child as a person in her own right. It will also increase your chances of helping your baby make whatever adjustments may be necessary to your family and to the world. Extremely active, demanding babies eventually have to learn to slow down a bit and to be able to wait to have certain of their needs met. On the other hand, parents of extremely quiet and adaptable babies must be careful not to overlook their babies' needs in the confusion of a busy household.

The development of a child is a two-way process—a complicated interaction between the baby, who was born with a distinctive disposition, and the people and experiences she encounters as she grows up. Your understanding and patience as parents will help your child accept the way she is and feel happy about it, while gradually learning that she is only one of the important individuals in the world. By taking this approach, you will be helping to show your child that people who are different can live together with respect and relative harmony.

Relating to a Newborn

People often talk as though newborn babies do nothing but eat and sleep. While this may be true of some newborns, your baby may have wakeful and alert periods as well. These times provide a good occasion for playing with her and getting to know her. She has some impressive sensory equipment: she can feel changes in temperature, distinguish tastes, smells, and voices. She is also very sensitive to touch and pressure. She likes skin contact and warmth, and is able to pick up your feelings about her from the way you relate to her. She'll respond well when you discover ways of handling her that are particularly appropriate to her temperament.[4]

Newborns can see objects that are six to twelve inches away (farther away they see only hazy blurs), and begin to distinguish between objects and people very early. Babies like to suck for comfort, and they like various kinds of comforting motion. Your baby may like to be rocked vigorously, bounced, or gently swayed or cuddled.[5] The human heartbeat may be soothing to her, or the rhythms of music, which, researchers have discovered, all tend to have the same range of beats as the human heart.[6] The research done to date is just a beginning in understanding what infants are really like. Realizing that research is incomplete may encourage parents to trust their own observations more and take an interest in new findings about infants.

The first step in knowing what to do with your baby is to watch her and be aware of what she is trying to do, what her signals mean. This is important because your baby is one of a kind, and because she is constantly changing as her perception of people and the world increases. So you need to pay attention to her and also to be willing to experiment. This way you develop the sensitivity necessary to pick up signals and think up ideas that might be fun or soothing. Knowing more about developmental sequences and temperament can also be helpful in understanding your baby.

As you get to know your baby, you will be increasingly aware of her favorite activities. Parents and babies discover their own games. For example, you lie on the bed with your knees propped up, and one day you try holding the baby on the top of your knees and sliding her down them like a sliding board, with appropriate sound effects. She obviously likes it—perhaps partly because of the fun of being suddenly closer to a familiar face, partly because she picks up the good feelings you radiate. This becomes something you do more often, because you both like it. Parents develop special ways of holding, carrying, and comforting their babies by a similar process of repeating the experiences that create mutually good feelings.

Remember to consider your own baby's temperament in choosing what is appropriate, and be aware that babies can be overstimulated as well as bored. Constantly overstimulating a baby will make her fussy and irritable, even though she seems to be enjoying herself at the time. Too much activity may set off a cycle of tension in her body that she is unable to break without your help. (See "Distracting and Soothing Your Baby," chapter 3, for ideas on helping babies unwind.) Babies need some quiet times when they can amuse themselves in their own ways. It is important to give them a chance to develop their own resources as they become increasingly able.

GETTING THE HELP YOU NEED
AS QUESTIONS COME UP

Finding a Doctor

Try to find a doctor who will be supportive in such decisions as circumcision and breast- or bottle feeding, and in attitudes toward crying and spoiling. The baby's doctor needs to have good medical qualifications first and foremost, but his emotional support can be very helpful as well. It is important that you feel comfortable talking with your doctor and that he is able to answer your questions in a way that helps you gain confidence as a parent. If you choose a doctor before the baby is born, you may feel more at ease during future visits. He will check the baby while you both are still in the hospital, and you can talk over any concerns you have about the baby or her care. If hospital policy permits, some doctors will leave explicit orders in the nursery regarding how soon after the birth you may see your baby, for example, or how frequently you may feed her.

If it turns out that your doctor is not supportive, you might seriously consider looking for another. Letting your doctor know why you feel his care is inadequate may help make him more sensitive to your needs and perhaps to the needs of other parents as well. Some doctors are very responsive to such confrontations; others aren't. You wouldn't hesitate to tell other professionals why you were dissatisfied with their services: doctors, too, need to know how their care is being received, and in what ways it is lacking. If you still don't get a satisfactory response, perhaps a friend who knows the kind of doctor you are looking for can recommend one more to your liking. Or, if you have confidence in your doctor's medical expertise and you don't want to make a change, you might decide to find the emotional support you need elsewhere, among family and friends, or from a Public Health nurse.

Don't be surprised if the doctor's nurse handles phone inquiries and routine well-baby care; the two of them are a medical team, and the nurse is probably familiar with much of the information you need. She may also be an experienced parent and more available than the doctor when you need help and advice. But when you really want the doctor's opinion or attention, you should feel free to insist on it. After all, you are paying for it. Find out what printed information regarding feeding, treating rashes, and so on, the doctor or nurse can give you to guide you through the first few weeks. Always be sure you write down any specific instructions (a small notebook for medical information might be a handy reference), so that later you still have the information at hand. Some doctors have specific times for phoning in routine kinds of questions. Ask what the procedure is for emergency care before you need such information and post it near the phone for you or a baby-sitter, should the need for it ever arise.

Supportive Friends
Sharing your feelings and ideas with supportive friends can be a valuable source of information and encouragement.

Friends who have recently had children and remember what new parenthood is like can be immeasurably reassuring. They can help you develop the confidence that you are doing a fine job and that your own feelings about how to handle your baby are often better than anyone's advice. Your friends may be able to give sympathy without being condescending when you are feeling low, and they can be living proof that you will survive and thrive as a family, even if things seem to be working out badly that particular day or week. You will probably discover by talking openly with them that they, too, had the same sorts of concerns and anxieties when they first became parents.

Other Community Services

There may be other services in your community that can provide additional help or support at little cost. For example, you may be able to call the Department of Health and arrange to have a Public Health nurse come to your home. If available, her visit will be free of charge. Don't worry about the house being a mess; Public Health nurses are well acquainted with the chaos surrounding the arrival of a baby. The nurse is apt to be a sympathetic listener and a good source of practical suggestions. The kinds of routine checks she does on both baby and mother can be helpful and reassuring, especially at first when you haven't seen your doctor yet. She can usually come back as often as you feel you need her—some willingly visit for as long as a year, or more. She is also apt to know of other services in your area that might be helpful to you.

In some areas local Public Health departments, free clinics (or women's clinics), hospitals, and medical schools have well-baby clinics where babies are given routine checkups, monthly at first, less frequently later. There may be a charge for this service, but if there is, it will be relatively low compared to the cost of regular visits to a private doctor. The atmosphere at clinics tends to be friendly and encouraging although you may have to wait and will probably see a different doctor each time. Most well-baby clinics do not treat sick babies, but could refer you to a doctor if you need one. Another way of saving money is to take advantage of the free immunizations given by the

Department of Health. You can do this even if you have a private doctor; most doctors accept your decision to make this arrangement while in their care.

PRACTICAL PROBLEMS

Finding Baby-sitters

Sooner or later every couple needs to get out of the house without the baby. Those who have relatives nearby often take advantage of their offers to baby-sit, especially at the beginning, but eventually new parents need to find non-family sitters as well. Unfortunately, many couples let finding a baby-sitter become such a great obstacle that it takes them forever to start looking seriously. For some reason parents of firstborns tend to feel that no one else will be able to care for their baby. Once you discover that there are competent baby-sitters who can be given the information needed to handle the situation, you will probably be surprised by how good it feels to get away on your own again—however briefly. It helps if both parents share the responsibility of finding a sitter and take turns making the phone calls.

There are many ways to go about finding a sitter. You can ask other parents in your neighborhood whether they know of any teen-agers who might be available and capable, and get their numbers. If you know a teen-aged baby-sitter who can't take on any additional families, ask her for the names of friends she would consider reliable and interested. If there is a college or university nearby, call and ask whether there is any way of contacting student sitters, or if you know any students, ask them for recommendations. If you know a teacher in the community, ask for names of students who might be interested in baby-sitting. Some high schools have lists of students who would like such jobs and will send names to inquiring parents. Check the Yellow Pages of your phone directory for baby-sitting services; you will have to pay more, but this is usually a reliable source for sitters. Or place an ad in the local paper. Asking for references in the ad or over the telephone is perfectly acceptable.

Once you have contacted a baby-sitter who seems promising

(and you can often tell much more than you expect by a phone conversation), arrange to have her come to your home to get acquainted with her. Let her see how you handle your baby, and tell her about any concerns you have, such as what you want her to do if the baby cries a lot. Be sure to make your expectations of her very clear and go over the baby's routine carefully. Being specific will make it easier for her and make you more relaxed about leaving. List emergency phone numbers, including the number of a nearby friend (and when you actually go out, the number where you can be reached). Show her where you keep first aid supplies, where any fire exits are, where extra clothing for the baby is kept, and anything else that might be needed. By this time you will probably know whether or not you feel comfortable leaving your baby with this sitter. If you still have hesitations, pay her for her time and ask for references or have her come back another day to get a second impression of her. It sometimes takes a teen-ager a little longer than an experienced adult to feel comfortable with an infant. Even if at first you aren't confident of her ability to handle the baby on her own, perhaps she would be able to take the baby for a walk while you take a nap or read a book. The fact that you have had her over and interviewed her does not obligate you to hire her for an evening alone.

Baby-sitting co-ops are becoming more widespread in towns, in apartment buildings, and in neighborhoods within cities. If there isn't one in your area, consider starting one among your friends and neighbors. Members of a co-op take turns sitting for each other. One person is bookkeeper and records the number of hours members sit for each other. This can be done using points or by using coupons with which parents actually pay each other. The job of bookkeeper can rotate among members, or the bookkeeper can be paid with extra coupons. There needs to be a policy about whether the sitter goes to the house of another family or stays home and has the children brought there. Groups need to be large enough that members aren't baby-sitting constantly and small enough so that some meaningful contact is possible among families. A co-op of fifteen to twenty families seems to work well.

There are other possibilities to investigate. Consider taking your baby (especially in the first few months) to a friend's home with a car bed or cushioned cardboard box to sleep in and an equipped diaper bag. Arrange to exchange baby-sitting with a friend who has children. This takes more of your time, but it is free and can be a lot of fun. When your baby is older, consider organizing a play group. By trading off children with three or four other mothers you can each have a few free mornings or afternoons a week. You can also check the Department of Social Services or the want ads of your local newspaper for lists of licensed day care homes and centers. A day care mother takes in children for some part of the day. Check to find out what the significance of licensing is in your state before you decide which kind of home to choose. These homes vary greatly in the kind of care they provide; by far the most important factor is the kind of person the day care mother is, so plan to visit any homes you are considering and stay a while. If you feel uneasy about any baby-sitting arrangement you encounter, remember that no on-the-spot commitments need to be made. You can say you are considering several alternatives, and you'll call when you've made a decision.

Getting Along with Grandparents

Your extended family may suddenly take on new meaning and importance when you have children of your own. You may feel a new closeness to your own parents, realizing what they must have gone through when you were a baby. But grandparents can also add problems to the lives of new parents. Since the support of a family is hard to replace, it is worth the patience and effort involved in trying to deal creatively with the problems that commonly come up with grandparents.

First of all, don't let grandparents divide you as a couple. You need each other, and there are already many ways in which you are being pulled apart. If you agree on the role you want the grandparents to play and agree on an approach to them, then you can stand together firmly and get your message across better. This will help you keep your sense of humor when the going gets rough and will keep resentment to a minimum. In fairness to everyone, you can't let grandparents interfere with your relationship.

Next you need to decide what kind of help you really want and need from grandparents (if they want to give it) and go ahead and spell out your needs, trusting that they would rather do really helpful things that are honestly appreciated than do what they think you want (or what they want) and be resented. If certain situations make you feel threatened—other people caring for your baby, visiting overnight in your home for an extended period of time, taking over your kitchen, or whatever —it is your responsibility to make it clear that you want them to keep hands off. Even if they make obvious hints that you are being silly or headstrong, you must ignore the hints and go ahead setting limits.

If dressing the baby, giving a pacifier, breast-feeding, or taking the baby outdoors become controversial subjects, as a couple you need to get your own feelings straight on these matters and then make your position clear and refuse to let them become issues of right or wrong. Such problems as how frequently grandparents should visit, whether you are spoiling your baby or not picking her up enough, or over-worrying about your baby's health should be handled with the firm conviction that you must work things out your own way. The fact is that the current beliefs about child rearing are different from those of a generation ago. If you continue to get advice that isn't appreciated, become skilled at casually changing the subject before you begin to get really angry. This is in no way disrespectful of your parents if you do it graciously; it is your way of establishing that you do not view yourselves as children in this setting but are adults with different opinions about how to handle a problem—your problem.

If you continue to have conflicts, you might try to include grandparents in activities that will help them understand your point of view. If your childbirth education group has a lecture on problems of new parents, consider taking your mother and/or father along. Show them a book on infant temperament and explain how much sense the theory makes to you. Take your mother along for your baby's checkup so she can see what your doctor's approach is and hear some open discussion of problems which may concern her. Invite your parents over when your friends with small children are there so they'll have a chance to talk with other parents your age. You may be surprised at their interest in these activities.

Occasionally grandparents don't seem interested at all. They may live nearby but lead very busy lives, leaving no time for you or your new baby. Try to be as tolerant of their life-style as you want them to be of yours. Don't take their casual approach as an insult, and continue to invite them to join your family as often as you wish. Then if they suddenly realize they are missing out on an important part of your lives—potentially of their own lives—they will be able to get involved with you again more easily.

Whatever your situation, if you are able to stick together and handle the problems that arise fairly consistently, there is a good chance that grandparents will respect your wishes and turn out to be very helpful and enjoyable to have around. Possibly they will even remember how they felt as new parents and suddenly appreciate with real sympathy what you are going through. They are apt to be more interested in the details of your baby's growth and development than anyone else and they may even be eager to baby-sit (be careful not to take unfair advantage of their offers); chances are they will be extremely thoughtful and caring of the baby, even if their style is different from yours. Grandparents are in the enviable position of being able to love and enjoy their grandchildren without having to assume total responsibility for them. Perhaps partly because of this unique relationship, children often grow to regard their grandparents as very special people.

Surviving in Cramped Quarters

If your house or apartment is small, you are apt to find that living on top of each other increases the tension and confusion that already surround you. But if you are thinking of moving, you should try to wait until the baby is several months old to avoid the mental and physical strain involved. Unless you must move, it is better to find ways to use the space you have more creatively.

Rather than use a full-size crib during the first few months of the baby's life, it makes sense to rely on something smaller. A portacrib, bassinet, carriage, or even a box or dresser drawer will probably meet your needs far better than a large crib. With a thin piece of covered foam inside, and a towel, for example, to cover the sides, the baby will be perfectly comfortable for a matter of months. Rather than buy a changing table, you can cover a piece of foam with vinyl or an old plastic tablecloth. When you want to change a diaper, put the pad on top of a low dresser, desk, or even on your bed. If all your diapering supplies are together in a portable box, the task of changing so many diapers will be less of a hassle.

Having to share your bedroom with your baby is apt to make you feel that you are never alone as a couple. As convenient as it may be to have the baby so close at hand when it comes to middle-of-the-night feedings, sharing your room for more than a month or so may be a situation you would like to avoid. Having an infant so near and hearing little noises all night may mean that you sleep less soundly and feel less rested in the morning. You may worry about waking the baby when you want to make love or talk in bed, especially if she has trouble going back to sleep. Also, feeling that you must pick up the baby at the sound of the first cry, so at least one of the adults can get some sleep, is not likely to encourage her to sleep through the night.

Some families have solved this problem by partitioning a room, thereby making a separate area for the baby. Or, if the baby is sleeping in a carriage, portacrib, or bassinet on casters, you can wheel it into a nearby room or around the corner when you go to bed. If you put a night-light in the next room, you can easily get there for nighttime feedings.

If you live in an apartment and your baby cries a lot, you may worry about disturbing the neighbors. Ask if they are bothered, and, if they do hear the noise, explain your problem briefly and tell them you hope that the crying periods will not last much longer. Even if there is no easy solution, at least they will appreciate your concern, and you may feel better after talking openly to them.

Make a point of getting out, with or without your baby, if you are starting to feel mentally and physically cramped. At times it may seem that packing everyone up to go out or finding someone to come stay with the baby is not worth the effort, but once you are out you'll discover that the benefits far outweigh the initial hassle.

Financial Considerations

Even if stretching a tight budget is not a new problem for you, it may become more frustrating when added to the other stresses you are under as new parents. This is a particularly annoying time to have to cut down on spending. You'd like to be able to afford whatever conveniences would make your lives as parents easier (diaper service, take-out meals, or whatever), and to go out for dinner or an evening and get a baby-sitter as often as you both feel the need. But with the essential equipment and clothing for the baby and medical expenses adding up, you may feel you must restrict your outside activities in order to pay the basic bills. (For suggestions of ways to save on medical expenses, see "Other Community Services" earlier in this chapter.) Your costs are undeniably greater now, and you may have to change your life-style a bit, but there are some ways to ease the pressure. With ingenuity you will be able to cover the baby's important needs without ignoring your own.

Sharing equipment and clothing. Hopefully you already know other families with young children. Passing equipment and clothing back and forth can work out to everyone's advantage in the end. Many baby things can also be bought secondhand. One baby doesn't usually wear out a crib, playpen, carriage, or car seat during the months she uses it. The same is true for a good many of the pieces of clothing that a baby wears. If you sew, once you can find the time you will be able to save money on clothes by using remnants and scraps of material. The baby clothes and equipment industry is quite a racket; figuring out how to beat it can be a worthwhile challenge. Keep in mind both ends of the cycle: getting things secondhand from some people and giving or lending your things to other people once you no longer need them.

Making simple toys. Toys can be shared or made. Washable ones can be purchased inexpensively secondhand. Garage and yard sales are excellent sources of used toys and baby equipment. Scraps of material can be used to make stuffed toys, and by combining different textures and colors you can create objects that are very appealing to young babies. Mobiles can be made by suspending colorful household objects from one or two wire coat hangers, and a piece of wide elastic can be used to suspend interesting but safe objects across the crib for the young infant to look at and the older baby to reach for. Pasting simple colorful pictures near where the child sleeps is another way of providing inexpensive sources of interest. Simple books can be made for the older baby by cutting out pictures of familiar objects, people, and animals and pasting them on heavy paper or cardboard. Older babies are also intrigued by ordinary household objects—plastic measuring cups, wooden spoons, pots, plastic tumblers, and containers for filling and pouring or making towers. Cardboard milk cartons and tin cans can be used for stacking and building. Empty spools of thread can be easily dropped into a wide-mouthed plastic bottle or coffee can by an older baby, and then dumped and filled again. A cardboard carton, decorated or plain, makes a good toy box.

The important guideline to follow when making or choosing toys is safety: Are all parts of the objects too large to be swallowed? Are none of its parts sharp to the touch? If painted, is the paint nontoxic? Test the toy by using the baby's own techniques for exploring it—mouth, fingers, etc. If you can't destroy it or be hurt by it, the baby probably can't either.

Inexpensive socializing and baby-sitting. There are many ways of getting out and seeing other adults without spending a lot of money. You can organize potluck dinners or picnics with friends or get together and bring your own drinks. Trips to museums, zoos, parks, local swimming pools, or lakes can also be inexpensive and fun. Many communities provide free or low-cost concerts, folk festivals, film festivals, or fairs. Keep your eyes open and you'll discover numerous possibilities.

To cut down on baby-sitting expenses, work out an arrangement where you exchange babies with friends in a similar predicament, either on a regular basis (once every other week, for example, so you can count on it) or now and then. Invite friends without children for dinner and then take them up on their offer to baby-sit sometime when you want to go out. Consider joining or organizing a cooperative baby-sitting pool as described earlier in this chapter.

RECOMMENDED READING

Aston, Athina. *How to Play with Your Baby.* New York: The Learning Child, 1971.

An excellent source of ideas about appropriate ways to play with a baby from birth to age two. Aston describes the developmental stages a baby goes through, suggesting how parents can make inexpensive playthings to intrigue their children at various points along the way. She includes an interesting growth chart that summarizes play ideas month by month, its only drawback being that it fails to emphasize that babies develop at different rates. Although Aston addresses only the mother in her book, both parents would probably find it interesting reading.

Brazelton, T. Berry. *Infants and Mothers.* New York: Dell, 1969.

In describing the behavior of three normal babies, Dr. Brazelton makes it extremely clear how different infants can be. He also shows how from birth these differences begin to determine the tone of the parents' reactions. By showing that a newborn affects his environment as much as it influences him, Brazelton hopes to alleviate the guilt parents might otherwise feel as they come into conflict with their infants. His descriptions of the interactions between average, quiet, and active babies and their families during the first year of life make worthwhile reading for new parents.

Caplan, Frank, ed. *The First Twelve Months of Life.* New York: Grosset and Dunlap, 1973.

Recognizing that parenting is a difficult job, Caplan has brought together much of the most recent research on infants in an effort to help parents understand why babies behave as they do. In addition to interesting descriptions of a baby's month by month development, the book contains numerous photographs and growth charts. Sensitive to individual differences among infants, Caplan is also sympathetic to the feelings of new parents. This book has a wealth of information which is both fun to discover and helpful to know.

Chess, Stella; Thomas, Alexander; Birch, Herbert G. *Your Child Is a Person.* New York: Viking, 1965.

Also stressing the uniqueness of each child, Chess et al. cover the years from birth to school age. In their description of temperamental differences, derived from a longitudinal study they did in New York, the authors convincingly demonstrate that raising children is a two-way process. The infant, born with a distinct temperament, affects his environment just as his environment influences him. Worthwhile reading for all parents, this book is a must for families with "difficult" babies, babies who react intensely to many or most of the situations they encounter and often seem to be screaming for a large part of the day. By relieving some of the guilt such parents may be feeling and by showing them how to work out a consistent way of handling their child, this book can help such families through an extremely difficult period.

Dodson, Fitzhugh. *How to Father.* Los Angeles: Nash, 1974.

A guide to the emotional and intellectual development of the child from birth to the age of twenty-one. Emphasizes the need for a man to learn about child psychology and successful teaching methods in order to be a good father. Encourages fathers to get involved with caring for and playing with their children from birth on. Includes five lengthy appendices, listing toys to buy, toys a father can make, children's books, children's records, and a survival kit for fathers (which lists books helpful in solving problems such as discipline, illness, sex education, divorce, drugs, etc.). Dodson should be commended for his attempt to get fathers involved in the important task of child rearing. Unfortunately, however, he only devotes ten pages to the entire first year of fatherhood.

Dodson, Fitzhugh. *How to Parent.* New York: New American Library, Signet, 1970.

Dodson stresses his belief that the first five years of a child's life are the most important in terms of both emotional and intellectual development. Emphasizing that parents are both teachers and child psychologists, he seeks to convey information that will make those jobs easier and more enjoyable. While many of his suggestions are insightful and useful, it is unfortunate that he wrote a book on "parenting" and yet addressed it only to the mother. To his credit, Dodson sympathetically reassures the new mother that it is normal to feel inadequate and resentful at times. And he admits that the continual crying of a colicky baby can make the parents feel frustrated, angry, and desperate. But he doesn't suggest how to cope with the situation, nor does he point out that some babies are temperamentally more difficult to live with. The five appendices are similar to those at the end of his newer book, *How to Father.* They include extensive lists of toys, books, and records that are appealing to young children, as well as an annotated bibliography useful to parents.

Fraiberg, Selma. *The Magic Years.* New York: Charles Scribner's Sons, 1959.

The Magic Years is full of insights that can help parents develop a fruitful way of thinking about problems that arise with their own baby. Fraiberg divides early childhood into three parts (birth to eighteen months, eighteen months to three years, three to six years) and then discusses typical problems and how to handle them in each developmental period. Fraiberg explores what mental health is and the role anxiety plays in normal development. She attempts to give insight into the mental life of the preschool child because she feels that most adults can't remember this time, and that adult intuition and imagination often fail in the face of problems presented by babies and young children. She emphasizes the importance of principles of child rearing that take into account both the facts of development and the expectations of our culture. Her book is fascinating to read, includes more theory than most (psychoanalytic in its orientation, presented openly for the reader to accept or not), and succeeds in giving a real sense of a young baby's world view.

Gordon, Ira J. *Baby Learning Through Baby Play.* New York: St. Martin's, 1970.

This "parent's guide for the first two years" contains numerous play activities for mothers and fathers to use with their babies and toddlers. The games are designed to help babies develop basic skills and to help them learn about their world. The activities are presented roughly in order of difficulty and require only the least expensive kinds of materials. Sketches are included throughout, depicting both fathers and mothers interacting with babies.

Spock, Benjamin. *Baby and Child Care.* New York: Pocket Books, 1968.

The quantity of useful information contained in this handbook is impressive. New parents will be informed and reassured by the clear descriptions and helpful suggestions that Dr. Spock has to offer regarding the physical and emotional development of a child. More than most authors writing for mothers and fathers, Dr. Spock expresses genuine sympathy for the difficulties new parents face and acknowledges the fatigue, anger, resentment, and ambivalence that are inevitable at one time or another. (A new non-sexist edition of *Baby and Child Care,* written with the needs of today's parents and children in mind, is scheduled for publication in 1975.)

U.S. Department of Health, Education and Welfare, Office of Child Development, Children's Bureau. *Infant Care.* Washington, D.C.: Superintendent of Documents, U.S. Government Printing Office, 1973. DHEW Publication No. (OCD) 73–15.

This seventy-two-page booklet can be ordered from the U.S. Government Printing Office for $.75. Though short, the book contains a great deal of helpful information for new parents. It covers such topics as basic care of the baby, special problems that may develop (such as illness or accidents), developmental characteristics of infants, ways to enhance their growth through play, and a discussion of temperamental differences among babies. The book is easy to read and refer to, and, though not nearly as comprehensive as Dr. Spock's book, it has the virtue of being short and including the basic information that new parents need.

U.S. Department of Health, Education and Welfare, Office of Child Development, Children's Bureau. *Your Child from 1 to 6.* Washington, D.C.: Superintendent of Documents, U.S. Government Printing Office, 1962. DHEW Publication No. (OCD) 73–26.

Available from the U.S. Government Printing Office for $.75, this ninety-seven-page booklet begins where *Infant Care* leaves off. It contains both medical and physical information, as well as material relating to the emotional and intellectual development of the child. In addition to presenting general developmental characteristics of children from the age of one to six, it makes helpful suggestions for handling special situations, such as going to the hospital, moving, handicaps, illnesses, and accidents.

3

Coping with a Crying Baby

The range of normal crying in newborns and small babies is very wide. But if your baby cries a lot, it may take you by surprise, especially if you have known other families with babies who seemed to sleep all day or were bright-eyed and cheerful when they were awake. Babies who are quiet and sleep much of the time are often referred to as "good" babies; so, by extension, you may wonder if you have a "bad" one or if you are inadequate as parents. These feelings, shared by many parents whose babies cry more than they had expected, will be stronger if your friends, family, or doctor avoid confronting the problem of crying and give you the impression that you should be able to deal with it on your own. If the crying persists and you have no outside support or relief, you may become alarmed at the intensity of your feelings of frustration and guilt.

There is no way to eliminate the problem of crying, but you may be able to reduce both the crying and your bad feelings by looking at the situation more objectively. It helps to understand as much as you can about the function and causes of crying in young babies. Experimenting with ways to respond to your baby may help you find an approach that not only alleviates some of the crying but also establishes a better relationship with her. Tips from other parents who have been more or less in your shoes can be very reassuring and can help you tolerate a less than ideal atmosphere without losing your self-confidence. You need to minimize the exhaustion, resentment, and anger you are both bound to feel at times. But you also need to help each other accept these feelings and realize they won't keep you from developing a positive relationship with your baby. If you continue to feel overwhelmed, you may want to get outside help from your baby's doctor or a counselor. Babies who cry with unusual persistence sometimes have special needs and require a special approach.

Just as you need more information about your baby to deal with the crying, you will find it helpful to think a little more about your own needs as parents in this difficult situation. You have to find a way of maintaining your sanity without feeling guilty and of learning not to expect too much of yourselves or the baby. This might mean getting outside help; it might mean trading off and getting away periodically. Certainly it will mean getting as much rest and reassurance as possible. Try to remember that the situation will improve with time. Fortunately, in many cases the worst of the crying has passed by the time the baby is three months old. Even if your baby's prolonged crying continues beyond three months, the chances are good that you will have begun to feel enough rewards from interacting with this intense little person to know that keeping your cool is worth the struggle.

WHY DO BABIES CRY?

The Function of Crying

It is important to realize that crying is, at first, your baby's only means of expressing her needs, of communicating physical or psychological discomfort, of asking for attention. Because of this, crying should not be simply ignored at the outset. You will want to try to understand your baby's messages and respond to her needs as much as possible. This will begin to teach her that she can communicate effectively. But sometimes babies continue to cry despite efforts to soothe them. Even though it may still be impossible to know for sure why your baby is crying or what you should do, it helps to understand more about the causes of crying and to know more ways of dealing with the problem.

Causes of Crying

You are not alone if you are unsure exactly what is causing your baby's discomfort. Doctors and researchers have many unanswered questions about newborn babies, and many of the ideas they have about crying are hypothetical or tentative. Here are some possibilities to consider:

Colic. If your baby cries a great deal, people are likely to say she has colic. There are conflicting popular reactions to colic. Sometimes a stigma is attached to having a colicky baby; it is supposed to reflect poorly in some way on you as parents. On the other hand, some parents are relieved if their baby is declared colicky because they feel it takes them off the hook and makes it clear that there is a physical cause, neither harmful nor lasting, for their baby's discomfort.

Although no one knows for sure what colic is, doctors think it is related to gastrointestinal discomfort which may be increased by the large amounts of air a baby draws in as she cries frantically. During a colic attack your baby will cry or scream, become red in the face, and probably draw up both legs in pain. These attacks may be moderate or intense and often last several hours at a time, frequently in the late afternoon or evening. Sometimes they are sporadic and unpredictable; sometimes they occur about the same time each day. Colicky crying usually tapers off by the time the baby is about three months old. Unlike a tiny infant who may have no means besides crying to release tensions or get rid of excess energy, a three-month-old can squirm around, play with her hands, concentrate on people and objects, make sounds, and perhaps even roll over.[1]

Since babies with colic often cry only after certain feedings, it doesn't seem to make sense to conclude that something is wrong with the milk you are giving your baby. Check with your doctor about this, however, because he may feel that making sure of the baby's diet is a good first step in dealing with the problem. Colicky babies tend to be healthy, hungry babies who drink a lot, gain well, and prosper physically.

In fact, part of the discomfort your baby feels could be caused by overfeeding. If she stuffs a fist into her mouth or makes sucking movements, you may conclude that she is hungry. And if offering her more milk restores peace and quiet temporarily, you may become tempted to feed her almost constantly. Food may be the answer if a couple of hours have passed since the last feeding; if not, it is a good idea to try another approach. Since sucking usually relaxes and comforts a baby, offering a pacifier or some water in a bottle might help. (If your baby isn't used to a nipple, you'll have to be patient and persistent.) Or perhaps, if you have already tried picking her up and soothing her without success, she may just need to be put down and left alone for a while. Once in bed, she may cry briefly and then settle down.

Tension. Prolonged and intense crying may lead to a buildup of tension in a baby. For example, although crying in a colicky baby is associated initially with eating, ingesting air, having gas, and drawing legs up tightly, other factors are apt to become involved if crying continues for a long period. Dr. T. Berry Brazelton, a pediatrician, describes the process this way:

> From a necessary three hours of crying, colicky babies begin to build up to eight or twelve hours a day. As they cry their entire body, including the intestinal tract, becomes tense and overactive. They gulp down air as they cry. Their stomach is sensitive to it and it creates pain, so they cry harder. As they pass the gas on through the rectum the pain persists, and so does the crying. Colic is usually blamed on the infant's gastrointestinal tract. I am convinced, however, that the physiological involvement is secondary to the build-up of tension in the whole body.[2]

On the other hand, crying may be your baby's way of releasing tension. In *The First Twelve Months of Life,* a baby is described who sooner or later reaches the point when no comforting seems to help for more than a couple of minutes. If the baby is put down to sleep, the crying that follows may be her way of unwinding and getting rid of excess energy.[3]

Regardless of the approach to your baby's crying you have chosen, it helps if you can be as relaxed and unruffled as possible. Your tension may have been set off by her crying and the frustration of feeling there is nothing you can do. But since you are all involved now, you can help by keeping the emotional pitch down. If you are tired and tense, your baby may become impossibly fussy and the situation will get worse. You may become overwhelmed and unable to keep perspective.

Remaining relaxed in the presence of a crying baby is extremely difficult, especially toward the end of the day when you are all apt to be tired, and your baby may be particularly fretful. If you find that day after day the tension around your home is steadily mounting as dinner time approaches, and the baby's fussing and crying are increasing, it really pays to take a few preventive measures. Think of ways to create a more relaxed atmosphere. Perhaps you could make dinner in the morning and then reheat it, take a break for some tea or beer, listen to some music, or take a late-afternoon walk. You might also consider the possibility that you aren't getting away from home enough. It is easy to see how hopelessly complex the situation is likely to become if you worry too much and feel tense yourselves. For more suggestions on how to deal with circumstances like these, see "Learn How to Break the Spiral of Tension at Home" in this chapter.

General physical discomfort. Sometimes babies need a little time before their bodies function smoothly, or they have some minor physical problem (a plugged tear duct, a rash, an allergy of some sort) that may cause temporary or long-term discomfort. These are the sorts of things that your baby's doctor will be on the lookout for when you go for regular checkups. All you can do is be patient, watch for and report any symptoms that seem unusual, and keep the schedule of well-baby checkups (including shots and vaccinations) suggested by your doctor or a well-baby clinic.

Overstimulation. So much has been written in recent years about the importance of stimulating young babies and exposing them to a variety of experiences that many new parents are not aware that babies can be overstimulated. Because babies are so different from one another, there is great variety in the amount of playing, noise, and exposure to new people and experiences that each can tolerate. Some gradual experimenting with your own baby will help you understand how much activity she can handle. If she is crying a great deal, or seems very wound up and extremely alert even when you know she must be tired, try less stimulation and perhaps more quiet time. The human mind is capable of being overloaded, just like a computer, and it reacts negatively.

Tiredness. The amount of sleep that babies need varies greatly, as does each baby's style of going to sleep. Some fall asleep easily when in the midst of noise and confusion, while others do better if they are left alone in a quiet place. Intense, active babies often have trouble unwinding and relaxing enough so that sleep is possible. Following a long wakeful period or an unusually stimulating playful time, a baby sometimes becomes so irritable that she simply can't stop fussing and crying. Trying to comfort such an infant with more talk or motion may make it even harder for the baby to fall asleep. Dr. Spock points out:

> Some young babies seem to be made in such a way that they can *never* drift peacefully into sleep. Their fatigue at the end of every period of being awake produces a tension that is a sort of hump they must get over before falling asleep. They have to cry. Some of them cry frantically and loudly. Then gradually or suddenly the crying stops and they are asleep.[4]

Infants who fuss more during the day seem to be more likely to sleep for long periods at night.[5] Since sleep needs vary with each baby, all you can do is try to be as aware as you can of your baby's sleeping patterns. Keeping these in mind and trying to get her onto a more regular sleeping schedule, if she is unpredictable, may help you minimize the frantic periods of overtiredness.

Loneliness. By the time she is several weeks old, your baby may be fussing because she is lonely and in need of company. You can meet this legitimate need for companionship without feeling you have to drop everything else you are doing. You might try putting her where she can see and hear what is going on. For more ideas, see "Distracting and Soothing Your Baby" in this chapter.

APPROACHES TO HANDLING A CRYING BABY

Picking up the Baby

Since babies need bodily contact and warmth to develop normally, responding to your baby's cries is a good idea. Worrying about spoiling her during the first few months is unnecessary. Studies have shown that responding fairly promptly to an infant's cries in the early months is less likely to encourage her to be demanding and dependent later on than delaying your response in the hope of avoiding spoiling.[6]

But what about the baby who keeps on crying even after being picked up? Does it do any good to continue to hold your baby if your comforting doesn't seem to help? If you feel relaxed and sympathetic toward her, there is a good chance she is picking this up and appreciating it. If holding your screaming baby is making you tense, irritable, and resentful, or if she has been picked up a great deal already and is wound up, continuing to hold her may only make matters worse. As you get to know her better, you will be able to decide which approaches make most sense for all of you.

Distracting and Soothing Your Baby

Another factor you need to consider when picking up your baby is the importance of broadening your approach as she grows and develops. The two of you will have to meet most of her needs in the beginning, but this will change as the weeks and months go by. It helps to be aware of the kinds of patterns you are establishing with your baby. If holding and feeding are the forms of soothing she has been led to expect most of the time, it will not be at all surprising if she becomes dependent on them for comfort. As the time goes on the patterns you establish may become limiting for both you and the baby. Rather than relying too exclusively on holding and feeding her, try to pick up her signals and interests. She may need a pat or rub on the back, a sympathetic word, a distracting toy, or a change of position. Possibly she needs to spend a little time alone occasionally when she is fussy. As you get to know each other better, you'll sense what is fair to expect. Have confidence in your baby and in yourselves and work on the problem slowly. You are apt to feel very rewarded by the new ways of relating you discover together.

As you begin to appreciate the variety of needs and interests your baby has, you may get some helpful ideas from the following suggestions made by experienced parents. You'll be adding your own ideas as you discover what is particularly helpful in distracting and soothing your own baby. Keep in mind that as your child grows she will develop new preferences, so if something fails to work today, try it again next week. Particularly if your baby is very fussy, you may be tempted to throw out ideas that don't work immediately; trying things frequently and with persistence is worthwhile if she is hard to soothe. Too many techniques in a short time, however, may confuse her and increase tension.

1. Motion: An automatic swing sometimes helps calm a crying baby. If she is tiny, try rolling up a towel on each side of her to support her head a bit and help her stay in a more comfortable position.

    Rocking chairs have the advantage of soothing both parent and child at the same time.

    Carriage (buggy) rides, indoors or out, or just jiggling a carriage while you sit in a chair can be soothing. Some strollers (such as the "Umbroller") are designed so that even a tiny baby can be propped up in them and enjoy looking around or even sleeping.

    Car rides are sometimes helpful in putting a baby to sleep. (Use a really safe car seat, such as the General Motors infant carrier or Peterson 75 model, if at all possible. If not, secure a car bed with safety belts in the back of your car.)

    Take a tour of the house, looking in mirrors, out windows, at colorful or interesting wall hangings or curtains.

    Go for a walk using a front pack or a backpack. Or use a baby carrier indoors, perhaps as you do some light housecleaning or prepare a meal.

2. Visual Stimulation: Objects that catch the light fascinate some babies, as will mobiles.

    Turning on a light near the baby may help, but for some babies even a night-light is too stimulating, and tends to make them stay awake longer when they awaken briefly at night. If there is nothing to see, they may go back to sleep.

Bright colors or interesting patterns near the crib, or soft balls, blocks, or animals will sometimes distract an infant. Colorful crib bumpers or pictures hung nearby are also worth trying.

Put a piece of wide elastic across the crib with a variety of safe, too-large-to-swallow objects on it: stiff plastic bracelets, strong rattles, empty spools of thread, cloth toys.

Prop the baby up in a buggy or an infant seat so she can see more. Or put her under a tree so she can watch the leaves gently moving in the breeze.

3. Rhythm and Sound: Sometimes more noise, rather than less, seems to soothe a fussy baby. Try turning on a radio or record player.

Wind chimes and musical mobiles and toys are often soothing.

Sing to your baby while you go about your work or take a break and play the piano or guitar with her nearby.

4. Freedom or Restraint of Movement: Some babies love to have all their clothes off and be free to move without restriction. Just lying on a blanket on the floor free to squirm and move about is soothing.

Others react strongly against such freedom. Swaddling such a baby very snugly in a blanket may help. When changing this sort of baby's diaper, try laying her on her back cushioned in a pillow for extra protection.

If your baby hates baths, it may be because of feeling unrestrained and insecure while in water. She may feel as though she is falling and startle backwards. Try wrapping her in a diaper or receiving blanket before you put her in the water. Then, after she is warm and wet, remove the blanket. Or hold your baby's arms securely (so she won't thrash around and scare herself) until she gets used to the water. A baby can be bathed in a plastic bath tub with only an inch or two of water in it. Roll up a towel for a head rest, and you'll have both hands free for holding and washing her.

5. Changing the Baby's Position: Your baby may get tired of being in the same position where she sees the same things. Turn her over or prop her in an infant seat or swing. Move her to a different room.

Colicky babies seem to be more comfortable lying on their stomachs, perhaps because the pressure helps relieve the gas.

Try laying your baby across your knees on her stomach and gently rubbing her back.

Some babies seem to enjoy lying on a hot water bottle (comfortable to the inside of your wrist, and then wrapped in a towel or diaper).

Pressure against your baby's feet can help her push if she is struggling with a bowel movement. Put her over your shoulder (with her stomach against your chest), and place one hand under her feet. If you prop yourself on a bed with three or four pillows behind you, you can relax in this position for longer periods of time.

6. Sucking: Try offering water to a baby who seems hot or thirsty between feedings or who has been crying and may therefore have taken in a lot of air. If your baby won't take plain water, add a little sugar or honey to it.

   Pacifiers can be very soothing to the baby who needs additional sucking but is not hungry. There are a variety of pacifiers on the market; if your baby refuses one type, it might be worth trying another. If possible, buy a pacifier which is molded in one piece since some have detachable nipples which may come loose and choke the baby. Do not put a pacifier on a string and place it around the baby's neck. To keep a pacifier close at hand, some parents find it helpful to pull a diaper halfway through the ring and rest it beside a sleeping baby's mouth. The bulkiness of the diaper tends to hold it in the right place.

   Some babies will take only the kind of nipple their bottle has. You can buy blind nipples, without holes, in drugstores and put them in the bottle collar or ring for a holder.

   Some nursing mothers discover that their babies want to suck beyond a feeding or between feedings, using the breast as a pacifier. Especially in the evening, when the mother knows she has virtually no milk, the baby can't overeat and feel miserable. If your baby refuses a pacifier, this may also be one of the few ways to help her relax if she is very active.

7. Helping an Overstimulated Baby Unwind: When you know your baby must be tired, even though she may not look or act tired, try not to bounce, jostle, or play with her in other ways that would stimulate her still further.

   If you finally get her to sleep and she wakes up again, keep any interaction or stimulation to a minimum, so she will not get wound up again.

   Rocking, walking, or even feeding your baby in a dark

room may help her unwind enough to go to sleep. Sometimes she may be so overtired and overstimulated that she will stay alert as long as she is handled in any way. In that case you may simply need to put her down and let her unwind and fall asleep by herself.

The process may take a while—up to an hour—but if you can feel your baby calming down, it is worth going slowly. Once you begin helping her unwind, it is important that you are not interrupted in any way and that you remain as patient as possible. If you try to rush things and put her down or leave the room before she is breathing heavily, with a limp and relaxed body, she may put up one last tenacious fight to stay awake. This is extremely frustrating; it becomes a battle of wills. Remember that it is worth a few more minutes to avoid such an exhausting confrontation.

You might try wrapping your baby tightly in a receiving blanket (swaddling her) so her arms can't thrash about, and so she can't push herself up in an attempt to keep on going forever. Then you can rub or pat her back gently. Once she realizes she can't move around, she may finally be able to fall asleep.

Holding a baby's bottom firmly with one hand and rubbing or patting her back gently with the other hand may help. Or sometimes holding her arms firmly helps her settle down.

Some of these suggestions may sound extreme to you. But if your baby is overstimulated and wound up, these techniques may be the kindest way to help her slow down enough to get some much needed sleep.

Letting the Baby Cry

What if your baby cries so much that you simply can't respond to all the crying without becoming exhausted and tense? Whether or not this happens will depend to a large extent on the amount of crying she does, how many people are sharing her care, and how much stamina and crying tolerance you have. If you view your situation as temporary, you may decide to dedicate yourselves full time to responding to your baby. But for many reasons this may not be feasable or sensible, especially if your attempts at comforting aren't reducing the crying, your baby is awake a lot, and if one adult is alone with her for long periods.

If your baby does a lot of crying, letting her cry may be one

of the most difficult things you have ever done. You may ago-
nize over the possibility that you are harming your baby and
feel guilty because you know something is bothering her and
you just can't find out what it is. You feel very reluctant to give
up and put her down to cry. But if you've done all you can,
putting her down is probably better than communicating a
great deal of tension and frustration.

It may be easier to let your baby cry if she has predictable
fussy periods each day that you are confident will end. Even
then, some parents become frantic if their baby's crying continues for more than a few minutes. It is hard to believe at first
that the baby might be better off crying for twenty to thirty
minutes than being picked up constantly after you have begun
to lose your sympathy and feel exasperated. Maybe letting the
baby handle things alone this time will make you more sympathetic another time, and your calmness will help decrease the
fussiness. Often parents report that the fussy periods gradually become shorter as they allow themselves to relax and the
general level of household tension decreases.

It seems only fair to point out that a baby who is continually
left to cry for long periods because of the frustration or apathy
of the parents is starting out life in a less than ideal way. Crying
is very often a baby's way of signaling for help; ignoring a large
portion of your baby's cries probably means that you are not
responding to her adequately. Parents sometimes feel such
strong anger that they suddenly understand what child batter-
ing is all about. Even if you don't come close to acting out this
anger, you may feel guilty about it. If you are bothered by this
kind of guilt or feel afraid you may act on your anger and hurt
your baby or yourself, call a crisis clinic, Parents Anonymous
group, Public Health nurse, or community mental health center. All you need to say is: "We are new parents, and we really
need help dealing with our baby—it just isn't working out."
Many parents feel this way, whether they admit it or not, and
you can be assured that your feelings are not unusual or peculiar. Parents who have negative and uncontrollable feelings
and are able to admit them and seek help usually come to feel
good as mothers and fathers. Not facing up to such feelings

can lead to severe problems later, possibly to child neglect or abuse.

WHAT TO DO IF THE PROBLEM PERSISTS

Check with the Baby's Doctor

If your baby continues to cry in spite of all your attempts at comforting, and your household is becoming increasingly tense as the days go by, you should see the baby's doctor. Even if an examination shows no definite physical cause for the crying, your doctor might well be able to suggest ways of coping with the atmosphere at home. Describe your baby's behavior as clearly as you can, and explain how it is affecting you. The doctor may only tell you that some babies simply fuss a lot; still, it is reassuring to know there is nothing physically wrong, and that you are doing all you can under the circumstances.

Your doctor may also offer you support in working out an approach that will ease the burden on you and relieve you of some of the guilt you may be feeling. Be honest about the direness of the situation if it is really serious. In cases of severe crying, when parents are thoroughly exasperated, doctors sometimes recommend getting away briefly, if at all possible, or prescribe a mild sedative for the baby or the parents. While you are not likely to find any magical solutions to the problem, you are entitled to as much reassurance and help as you need to get through these difficult weeks.

If your doctor is unable to give you support, remember that anyone who has not had the experience of total responsibility for an infant who cries a great deal may honestly not understand the intensity of your feelings and frustration. Your situation is very difficult and you need an understanding ear. If your doctor can't help, find someone who can. (See "Getting Outside Help and Support" in this chapter.)

Learn How to Break the Spiral of Tension at Home

Anyone who has lived with a baby who cries a lot will recognize the degree of tension that everyone feels if the crying goes on and on. Sooner or later you feel angry, resentful, and even desperate. It is difficult to get rest and hard to convince your-selves that nothing is wrong with your baby, even if you have consulted closely with your doctor. It is equally hard not to blame yourselves and feel annoyed with each other. None of your superhuman efforts to comfort your baby have brought about the desired results. Dr. Spock describes the feelings of the parents of a crying baby who is impossible to soothe:

> He not only refuses to be comforted—he acts as if he were angry at you for trying. These reactions are painful for you. You feel sorry for him, at least at the beginning. You feel increas-ingly inadequate, because you're not able to do anything to relieve him. Then as the minutes go by and he acts angrier and angrier, you feel that he is spurning you as a parent and you can't help feeling mad at him underneath. But getting angry at a tiny baby makes you ashamed of yourself, and you try hard to suppress the feeling. This makes you more tense than ever.[7]

If you are all caught up in a spiral of intense feelings, it is important to re-establish some calm. How do you do it? The challenge you face is working out a reasonable approach when you are not under stress and then carrying it through when a crisis occurs. If you take the same approach each time, your baby will gradually learn what to expect from you. Once you get a pattern established, follow it through with confidence. The approach itself may be less important than the calm deter-mination with which you carry out your plan. Even if you can't control the baby's behavior or stop the crying, you can get a grip on your own feelings and by doing so communicate less anxiety to your child. Dr. T. Berry Brazelton describes a tense situation where he tried to help new parents develop a worka-ble plan of action:

> Mrs. Crane was distraught, weeping, and I could barely gather the details of the problem. Apparently she had not slept for thirty-six hours; Lucy had been crying off and on most of that time, looking around for short periods when she wasn't crying. Whenever Lucy slept, and even when she was awake, she would startle and then begin to cry with loud, piercing wails.

Mrs. Crane described how the three adults in the household —her husband, her mother, and herself—would rush in to the baby and frantically institute a long series of efforts to quiet her down. Lucy would refuse a pacifier. Carrying her and rocking her quieted her briefly, but she started again if the motion stopped. Swaddling her made her angrier. She spat out sugar water and had begun to refuse any bottle offered her. If she were put to breast, she sucked briefly, choked and turned away after a few minutes to wail again. As the tension in the family built up, Lucy's crying became more frequent and more persistent. When she did sleep it was only in short bursts. . . .[8]

Dr. Brazelton urged everyone to get more sleep and try to relax. Then he begged all three adults to stop their frantic fussing over Lucy:

I assured them it was not as hard on her to cry for periods of fifteen or twenty minutes at a time before being picked up as it was to be jostled and held with no message coming across but one of frantic tension. I assured them that if she cried in short bursts, was given water and bubbled periodically, the water would mobilize whatever air she had cried down and sucking on the bottle would quiet her. I asked them to set up just such a routine when she was colicky—twenty minutes of crying, ten minutes of sucking and comforting, twenty minutes more of crying, and so on. They were to keep a log of the day and call me each afternoon to report on the crying.[9]

Brazelton reports that within five days Lucy's crying was organized into two predictable periods: one hour in the early morning and two hours at suppertime. As the parents became less frantic and tense, so did Lucy.[10]

In the face of your exasperation it may be difficult to come up with any plan of action. Now it may help to sit down together with a cup of coffee and talk over your frustrations. If you feel guilty about being angry with your baby, you may be keeping your emotions inside. Expressing these feelings and talking about them together instead of internalizing them may make you both feel better and help you find the energy and confidence you need to plan a way out of your dilemma. Even if you aren't sure exactly what to do next, you'll probably feel closer and less worried about how you'll be able to end the crisis.

Find Out More about Unusually Difficult Babies

Some babies are born with a combination of temperamental qualities that make them unusually intense and difficult to handle. The research of Drs. Chess, Birch and Thomas on infant temperament has shown that one out of ten babies is born this way.[11] While many babies have extreme reactions from time to time, difficult babies have them frequently—it's a matter of degree. You may recognize your baby in some of these descriptions:

> Their habits are irregular. They don't establish definite hunger and sleeping patterns that are predictable from day to day. They don't have bowel movements regularly. They tend to have negative withdrawal reactions to most new stimuli and situations. In addition, they are not easily adaptable, and almost every change in their routines involves a struggle.
>
> Their moods are predominantly negative. Unlike the average five-week-old baby who begins to smile and wriggle when a stranger playfully dangles a rattle above him, the negative child may turn away and start howling. The reactions of such youngsters are also frequently intense. When they cry, they often bellow; and their laugh, too, is loud and long.[12]

The intensity that such babies show often elicits equally intense responses from their parents. It is very important to remember that these babies are not deliberately trying to give their parents a hard time. If your baby is difficult, she needs your sympathy; her intense feelings and crying are hard on her as well as on you. But if you allow yourselves to feel sorry for her, you are apt to feel guilty about carrying out the firm approach that such babies need. This may make life harder for all of you and result in resenting your baby rather than feeling sympathetic toward her.

Babies who are difficult seem to need the extra help of knowing exactly where their parents stand. But this is only one side of the problem. What you need, as the parents of a difficult baby, is a fair way of limiting your efforts without feeling

guilty. You want to avoid a pattern in which you knock yourselves out trying to comfort your baby and then, when your
efforts appear to be fruitless, you feel like knocking your baby
out to comfort yourselves. When you fall into this kind of a
pattern, you are upset and trying too hard, and you are giving
confusing messages to your child as well. Sticking to a consistent plan of action will give you more predictable and regular
expectations of yourselves and your baby. This will help you
relax more and will gradually help your baby to change.

It is difficult to plan a routine when you don't see changes
overnight, but parents who have tried this approach have
found that results do come with time. Gradually the intense
crisis atmosphere settles down to a predictable routine where
the whole family seems happier and more able to enjoy one
another. Exactly how you plan your routine will depend on
your baby and your own needs. You might start by keeping a
running account for several days of your baby's activities
(sleeping, eating, crying, playing, reactions to various situations) and of your own reactions as well, if possible. Then look
at it and try to figure out how to make your baby's schedule
more regular, deciding on rest or nap times, bed times, feeding times and play times which grow as much as possible out
of the pattern she already seems to be developing. The hard
part is carrying out your plan consistently for a week or two,
when you may feel you have very little to go on at first. But by
then you'll be able to reassess your situation, see what changes
have occurred, and decide whether to stick to your present
plan or make a new one.

The extra effort you are expending may make you lose perspective now and then—you are only human. The real rewards
you feel from working with your child in this way may be well
in the future, as they were in the case of Roger's family, reported by Chess et al.:

> Roger's father was pleased to have such a "lusty" youngster.
> He cheerfully told us how loud and long Roger howled with his
> first baths, new foods, strangers, and vaccinations. But the fa-
> ther knew Roger would always settle down eventually, "and

then he's such a pleasure." The mother was not so sure this lustiness was a virtue. She was periodically uneasy and guilty, felt she must be a bad mother, and even became mildly depressed over Roger's recurrent crying and difficulties with sleeping and feeding.

But her husband not only reassured her; he pitched in with the care of this difficult child. This helped the mother maintain a patient, consistent, and positive approach. The parents were rewarded as Roger became a toddler and then a schoolboy.

His adjustment to routines became increasingly smooth, his behavior showed fewer negative reactions, and he did indeed become a lusty, exuberant youngster.[13]

Your job is bound to be difficult, but your active and demanding baby has a forceful and expressive personality which you will gradually come to appreciate. If you succeed in maintaining a basically friendly atmosphere and in carrying out your routine in a patient way, your baby will eventually cry less and you will begin to see improvement in the situation at home. You can't expect yourselves to be perfectly consistent when your job is hard and change is slow. That is why you can be of so much help to each other, encouraging each other and keeping up each other's enthusiasm when life with this intense baby seems exhausting. When you let your baby cry, keep reminding yourselves that you are doing it for a reason. You're a long way from the frantic crisis you were beginning to find yourselves in and the exhausting ups and downs you might otherwise have experienced. If you are unscheduled people yourselves, you may find it hard to follow these recommendations, but they are worth trying for two or three weeks. Then you will either be convinced of the benefits or you will decide that the effort is not worthwhile.

Consider Limiting Visitors and Outings

It is hard to establish and stick to a routine when you have a steady stream of visitors. Unless they are very close and sympathetic friends, they might misunderstand or disapprove of what you are trying to do with your baby and inadvertently undermine your efforts in some way. And having extra people around when you are living with a crying baby is apt to make you feel more tense and guilty. Furthermore the extra household commotion may make your baby become over-stimulated. It may really help in the long run to discourage visitors other than your closest friends until you can establish a pattern with your baby that leads to less crying.

The same is true of taking the baby out frequently, especially to places where there are many people and a lot of noise and confusion. It is fine for you to be in these situations—it may even help you—but unless you arrange a baby-sitter for your baby, you may discover that the disadvantages outweigh the benefits. Just when your baby finally seems to have settled into a sane routine, a noisy outing or gathering may disrupt the calm you have worked so hard to establish. The result may be that for the next two or three days or nights her routine is shot, she isn't satisfied with anything and doesn't eat or sleep well. So keeping your social life as low-key as possible, or getting a sitter when you want to go to parties or other big events, is probably the best approach. Eventually you may decide you want to help your baby learn to handle all the kinds of fun that you enjoy, but until you have the confidence that you can re-establish a consistent pattern with her in the aftermath of these experiences, taking her may be self-defeating.

YOUR OWN NEEDS ARE IMPORTANT TOO

Taking your own needs seriously is as important as considering those of your baby. Understanding how each of you is reacting to the other and to the baby may help you sort out what is happening. Some parents find it worthwhile to take a look at their own characteristic responses, particularly those that relate to how they react under pressure.

The point is to think about how your responses might contribute negatively or positively to your circumstances. When you are under stress, for example, do you withdraw, become frantic, blame yourself, get angry at others? Each of your reactions affects your partner in various ways. One of you may get very upset when anyone cries and actually feel quite helpless. If so, you may have to make a special effort to get away from

the crying or learn how to relax with it; otherwise you won't
be able to help stick to a schedule. Perhaps one of you is more
irritable than the other when awakened in the middle of the
night or early in the morning. One of you may be more persistent and can take the lead in getting a routine going.

The chances are that you will find you can modify your own
responses in order to work together toward an approach that
leads to improvement. But don't expect yourselves to change
overnight, and do remember to take your own needs into
consideration. Especially if you are trying to establish a routine
with an intense child, you must think about how all three of
you function best.

You Both Need to Get Away

One of the most difficult tasks you face is remaining calm in
an emotionally charged atmosphere. Many parents with difficult babies get stuck at home, but for everyone's sake, you
should avoid this pattern. You deserve a break, and you need
to know that others can handle the situation for a few hours.
As Dr. Spock points out:

> You should make a great effort to get away from home and baby
> for a few hours at least twice a week—oftener if you can arrange
> it. Hire someone, or ask a friend or neighbor to come in and
> relieve you. If you're like most people, you hesitate to do this.
> "Why should I inflict the baby on somebody else? Besides, I'd
> be nervous being away from him for so long." But you
> shouldn't think of a vacation like this as just a treat for you. It's
> very important for you, for the baby and for your husband that
> you do not get exhausted and depressed. If you can't get any-
> one to come in, let your husband stay home one or two eve-
> nings a week while you go out to visit or see a movie, and
> encourage him to take one or two nights off a week. The baby
> doesn't need two worried parents at a time to listen to him. Try
> also to get friends to come in and visit you. Remember that
> everything that helps you keep a sense of balance, everything
> that keeps you from getting too preoccupied with the baby,
> helps the baby and the rest of the family in the long run.[14]

To keep up your strength and to renew your energy and
stamina, you both need to get away. Right from the beginning,

take turns staying at home so each of you can get out for a while. Then try to find someone you can trust (a relative, friend, or experienced baby-sitter) to carry out whatever approach to handling your baby you have decided on. Emphasize how strongly you feel about what you are doing. The person caring for your child will probably feel reassured by your clear-cut advice. If you feel better about it, stay away for only short periods. Just getting out and becoming involved briefly in other matters with other people will help tremendously. Each of you needs outside relationships with adults you enjoy and care about to reinforce your ability to weather the crisis you are in.

Sleep Is Also Essential

Getting enough sleep helps you cope effectively, so it is crucial that you try to figure out a way to do just that. You can put an extra mattress on the floor beside your bed and feed the baby there. When she goes back to sleep, either stay there with her or move back into your own bed. If you have a rocking cradle, you might try attaching a long string to one side of it. When the baby fusses at night, between or after feedings, pull the string to rock the cradle. Putting her to sleep in a buggy near your bed and then reaching over to jiggle it gently when the fussing begins has the same effect. But if bringing the baby into your room means that none of you gets a good night's sleep, these may not be sensible ideas. Maybe you need to take turns being "on call." If necessary, one of you can sleep somewhere else, in the living room or even in a sleeping bag in the basement, away from the night's distractions. Turning on a fan might provide just enough background noise to allow you to relax more completely. If your sanity and ability to cope are at stake, you might buy some ear plugs and take turns using them.

Getting Outside Help and Support

By this time you probably have a fairly good idea of the kind of support you can get from your baby's doctor. You may want to let him know how you are doing and explain your approach briefly; he may be able to make further helpful suggestions or may wish to stay in touch with you as you work things out.

If you find that you are simply unable to cope with the crying on your own, think seriously about getting additional outside help. Try to find someone who has had experience with the pressures new parents are under to help you get back on the right track. A Public Health nurse, who makes free home visits if you call the Department of Health and arrange for them, can sometimes offer this kind of assistance. Or perhaps you would benefit from seeing a counselor. Even one or two sessions with a family counselor can be a tremendous help if you have lost your perspective. Perhaps there is something you have overlooked that would be obvious to someone with a more objective eye and a lot of experience with such problems. Maybe just explaining what you are going through will help you see for yourselves how to go on together.

THERE ARE NO EASY ANSWERS

You Have to Find Your Own Way

All the advice in the world about how to handle your crying infant will be useless unless you feel comfortable with it. The most you can do is to consider the pros and cons of the various approaches, including any that you have discovered on your own. Then choose whichever seems best to you. You may be surprised by some of your own reactions. Just when you feel you have things straight, you may start to vacillate and again begin to feel immobilized by your situation. Unfortunately there are no easy answers with guaranteed results. If you succeed in the first three months in finding an approach you are happy with most of the time, then you have done well. Don't expect miracles, and don't be too hard on yourselves if all your problems don't vanish and you still feel frustrated and disappointed from time to time.

Anger and Frustration Are Inevitable

Deciding on an approach together may help you avoid one of the major problems that can develop: blaming yourself or each other for the difficulties. Anger, with its underlying feelings of sadness, loneliness, inadequacy, or fear, is particularly hard to deal with in your situation because there is no good place to direct it. Try to learn from these feelings, rather than blame yourselves for having them. See whether you can figure out what triggers them: being alone too much with the baby, not getting enough rest, or losing touch with each other as a couple? If you can share your angry feelings with each other rather than direct them at each other, or at the baby, you will probably be better off. You need to get the anger out, but if you direct it at the people you love, you may end up feeling worse. Getting information, making decisions, and attending to the details of the routine may help you work through some of your anxiety and ease your frustration. But nothing is going to take away the strong feelings you are experiencing, so help each other express and accept them as much as you can.

The Future Will Be Brighter

When you feel low, you must keep reminding yourselves that things will improve with time. You'll still go through days that seem impossible, but as your baby gradually learns to adapt to new situations and experiences, she will have fewer hurdles to cross and will have learned a great deal about what your expectations are. And as you relax and enjoy your baby more, you'll probably realize that you are moving ahead little by little, and you'll begin to see the more rewarding side of parenthood.

RECOMMENDED READING

Caplan, Frank, ed. *The First Twelve Months of Life.* New York: Grosset and Dunlap, 1973.

See "Recommended Reading," chapter 2.

Chess, Stella; Thomas, Alexander; and Birch, Herbert G. *Your Child Is a Person.* New York: Viking, 1965.

See "Recommended Reading," chapter 2.

Spock, Benjamin. *Baby and Child Care.* New York: Pocket Books, 1968.

Especially useful and sympathetic is Dr. Spock's section on "Crying in the Early Weeks," pp. 183–91.

4

The Breast-feeding Decision

For many women the breast-feeding decision is complicated by popular attitudes which put it out of focus. Nursing your baby is not a test of your femininity, nor is it necessarily a measure of your commitment to motherhood or to your baby.[1] On the other hand, nursing is not alien to your femininity; it is an aspect of female sexuality and a uniquely female experience that a woman should seriously consider exploring firsthand. Moreover, it may become an intimate part of your commitment to your baby. Breast-feeding is a skill which usually takes time to learn. It is flexible enough to meet the needs of many kinds of mothers, babies, and fathers.

The great majority of women in this country bottle feed their babies;[2] at least some of them do this not because it is what they really want, but because they don't have adequate information and support. The more you know about breast-feeding, the more likely you are to succeed at it. But whether or not nursing turns out to be a pleasurable experience also depends on factors you can't control.

The goal of this discussion is to deal openly with the difficulties you may encounter, while still providing the kind of information that will help you find satisfaction in breast-feeding. You should take the time to decide as a couple whether or not it seems right for your family and support each other no matter how it works out for you. If you decide to breast-feed, don't let the attitudes of others interfere with your success. You should feel free to choose a style of nursing that meets your particular needs. The fact that a woman wants to combine motherhood with other involvements, or that a couple is sharing parenthood and outside work doesn't preclude nursing, though it may pose some problems. If you decide against breast-feeding, or if you wean your baby earlier than planned, you can go ahead with bottle feeding without fearing that you have failed in some way or that your baby will suffer as a consequence. Your feelings about your baby and yourselves are far more important than the way you feed her.

BOTH PARENTS ARE INVOLVED
IN MAKING THE DECISION

In some families, both parents are in favor of breast-feeding and have few reservations about it, while in others, bottle feeding is the only method seriously considered. Since a baby can thrive both emotionally and physically with either method of feeding, each family is right in feeling confident and comfortable with their decision. Other parents feel unsure of what they want to do and waver between the two approaches. Many new mothers would like to try nursing but have moments of doubt. Will there be enough milk? Is it possible to feel comfortable nursing in front of relatives and friends? New fathers sometimes feel uneasy about nursing too. They may wonder whether the intimate nature of breast-feeding will make them feel left out. Some new fathers would like to participate in feeding the baby but feel they cannot be involved if breast-feeding is the method chosen.

If you are wavering, consider giving nursing a try. If you have adequate information and are open about your feelings, none of you can lose from a short breast-feeding experience. And once you are involved, your feelings and doubts are apt to be resolved, one way or another. You can always stop breast-feeding, or decide to combine breast- and bottle feeding if that seems best.

If you are seriously considering breast-feeding, it makes sense to find out about the mechanics of milk production, to know the common problems nursing mothers have, and to consider the possible styles of breast-feeding and how they might meet your needs. Since doctors are frequently unfamiliar with certain aspects of breast-feeding, new mothers are not always able to rely on them for helpful advice or factual information. Close friends who have nursed successfully can be a source of encouragement and helpful suggestions, but their experience will necessarily be different from your own. Other sources of information include books about breast-feeding, hospital and Public Health nurses, childbirth instructors, and La Leche League International.

La Leche (pronounced lay-chay, the Spanish word for milk) League is an organization of nursing mothers with local chapters all across the country. Pregnant women who are planning to nurse and mothers already breast-feeding are welcome at the regular meetings of the local chapters, and any woman with nursing problems is encouraged to call the league's telephone number, whether or not she belongs to the group. The league's purpose is to help you solve nursing problems. If you want to know how to nurse while your baby is ill, need help finding a breast pump, or have questions about breast infec-tions or sore nipples, the league can provide unlimited sup-port. But if you need help in deciding whether or not to con-tinue nursing, or how to combine bottle and breast-feeding to meet your particular needs, the league may not be the best place to call. Since traditionally their views have supported only breast-feeding totally, without supplementary bottles, you might find their attitude limiting or intimidating. Some chapters of the league may differ from this approach; you can check by calling and bringing up the question. For further information about the chapter nearest you, write to La Leche League International, 9616 Minneapolis Avenue, Franklin Park, Illinois 60131.

As you make your decision, it is important to keep in mind how much the nursing experience differs for each woman and each couple. Some mothers have fantastic support from those around them; others are not so fortunate. Some have beauti-fully cooperative babies who nurse easily and conveniently; others have babies who seem to be constantly dissatisfied, making it hard to relax and enjoy the feedings. For some women breast-feeding causes little or no soreness, while for others it turns out to have unexpected discomforts. When unforeseen obstacles arise, parents need to support each other and talk openly about their feelings. Fathers can be extremely helpful in encouraging their wives to relax and stop worrying, and a father's willingness to take over chores that have not been done can make it possible for a nursing mother to get the rest she needs. He can give emotional support to his wife if she meets with disapproval or unappreciated questioning from relatives and acquaintances.

But a woman needs to be sensitive to her husband's feelings in this situation as well. Even if he basically supports nursing, he may get discouraged and frustrated if problems with nursing continue and he feels he must stand helplessly on the sidelines. He may feel he is being called upon too much to be supportive and helpful and start to feel tired and depressed himself. Or he may begin to feel that the time his wife must spend with nursing problems makes it impossible for her to get enough rest or spend enough time with him. These are all legitimate and understandable feelings, and they need to be expressed. In fact, breast-feeding can be very tiring and time-consuming in the beginning. (Actually, babies can be very tiring and time-consuming, no matter how you feed them.) But both parents need to remember that the first few weeks are the most demanding and that the situation will gradually improve. You must take into account the amount of strain each of you is under and how strongly each of you feels. No one can consider your circumstances more fully than you can; what you do is your decision, and you should not let well-meaning friends or relatives make it for you.

All mothers who try nursing need and deserve support. And once the flexibility of breast-feeding is recognized, women can go on to pay attention to their own experience and their own feelings, and decide with their husbands whether to nurse, how to nurse, and when to stop nursing, confident that any decision they make can turn out well and any amount of breast-feeding can be worthwhile. This chapter by no means contains all the information you are likely to need if you nurse, but hopefully it will be a helpful beginning.

MYTHS AND FACTS ABOUT BREAST-FEEDING

Sickness and Allergies

Breast milk seems to have some anti-infective qualities and does contain antibodies against some viruses and bacteria. But in our country, where sanitary conditions generally prevail, there is no demonstrable difference in infection that can be positively related to feeding method.[3] Breast-feeding may be a wise choice for families with a history of highly allergic reactions. But since findings about the advantages of breast milk over cow's milk formulas in preventing allergies are somewhat out-of-date because of the newer commercial formulas, studies need to be repeated.[4]

Closeness of Mother and Baby

All of the evidence indicates that the method of feeding is less important in the emotional well-being of a baby than the kind of relationship that is developing between the parents and the child.[5] Positive early feeding experiences contribute to the development of a well-adjusted child, but the method of feeding is only one of many factors to consider. Skin contact may (but need not) be an important difference between the two methods. Strong feelings of maternal (or paternal) closeness are an aspect of any good feeding experience.

Convenience and Cost

There is no significant difference between the convenience of nursing and of bottle feeding if you can afford today's disposable, ready-made formula.[6] Convenience is partly a matter of how comfortable you feel with the method you have chosen. Both methods can be convenient, but the cost of formula is greater.

Fussiness and Crying

It is worth checking with your doctor to try to establish a link between what your baby is being fed and any discomfort she may be feeling; fussing and crying, however, are more likely to be caused by other factors than by feeding. (See chapter 3.)

Nursing in Public

Nursing in public is still considered inappropriate by some although this attitude seems to be changing somewhat as mothers combine outside involvements or professional life with mothering and discover the flexibility of nursing. If a woman feels more comfortable being discreet, she can use a shawl, sweater, or small blanket as a cover-up, or she can go to a ladies' lounge or her car for more privacy.

Effect on Mother's Body

Nursing helps your uterus return to normal more quickly; contractions of the uterus are stimulated by the baby's sucking.[7] The return of menstruation will probably be delayed for part or all of the time you are nursing. Sometimes your skin and hair are less oily. Some studies also show that nursing for long periods (up to a year or more) is associated with a decrease in the likelihood of getting breast cancer.[8] Ask your doctor for the latest thinking on this point.

For some women breast-feeding is sexually stimulating and pleasurable, feelings for which many women are unprepared. In our culture a distinction is often made between maternal and sexual feelings.[9] In fact, many parents discover a compatibility between these feelings, and nursing may be one experience that makes the connection more clear. (See "Nursing and Sexuality" in chapter 5.)

Breast Changes

Your breasts will be fuller while you nurse. Uncomfortable fullness and leaking usually diminish after the first few weeks of nursing. You can stop the leaking by applying pressure to your breasts with the heel of your hand when you feel milk begin to flow. If your breasts are greatly enlarged, it is important to wear a well-fitting bra—day and night—to prevent stretching of the skin and the supporting tissues. Some women find that their breasts return to their usual size after weaning; others find that their breasts stay larger or seem smaller. Droopy breasts are not caused by nursing. Many women notice a change in their breasts after childbirth, but this is caused by pregnancy, not lactation, and the extent of the change is determined by heredity, age, and the amount of weight gained in pregnancy. The idea of "used" breasts, rather than breasts that are purely erotic and and "belong" to the man, scares many women and men away from breast-feeding.[10] Couples who have previously seen the breasts as primarily erotic may find that it takes a while to sort out their feelings about nursing a baby and how nursing relates to parenthood and sexuality.

Gaining Weight

Nursing does not need to cause weight gain. A nursing mother should eat about a thousand extra calories a day, but if she is careful in her choice of foods and exercises moderately, this will not make her gain weight.[11] Most books on breast-feeding include recommendations about the diet of nursing mothers. Diet is important but need not be complicated. Some nursing mothers feel constantly hungry. Others discover that they can eat tremendous amounts without gaining weight.

BREAST-FEEDING IS A LEARNED SKILL

Misinformation about breast-feeding is so common that it is not unusual for pregnant women and new mothers to have unrealistic or inaccurate ideas of what the experience will be like. The fact that it is the natural way to nourish a newborn does not mean that you will automatically know how to nurse your baby or feel comfortable doing it. Breast-feeding, like many other aspects of parenthood, is a skill that takes time to master. Don't expect instant success or enjoyment. It will probably take a while for you to get used to nursing and to feel confident as a nursing mother.

For the first couple of weeks you are apt to feel tenderness or pain as your nipples get used to your baby's frequent sucking. Leaving your nipples exposed to the air as much as possible and not using soap as you wash your breasts during the last trimester of pregnancy as well as during the nursing period will help toughen them up. Also, using your fingers to roll and pull your nipples, as described in many books about breast-feeding, can be helpful.[12] Increasing the baby's sucking time gradually, from a few minutes at each breast at the begining to as long as ten or fifteen minutes by the second week or so, will give your nipples a chance to toughen up little by little.[13] When you move the baby from one breast to the other, be sure to break the suction of her mouth on your nipple first by inserting a finger at the place where she is sucking. Otherwise you are likely to feel pain.

As your nipples are toughening, your body is adjusting to the stimulation of your baby's sucking and is beginning to supply the amount of milk that she needs. Feeling engorged at first is almost inevitable, and the feeling may continue on and off as your baby begins to sleep for longer periods. Waking up in the morning feeling overfull is common. Some women find that letting their milk begin to flow (by placing a warm washcloth on their breasts) before the baby starts to nurse decreases the painful sensations of the first few seconds and prevents her from choking on the initial swallows. Nursing your new baby whenever she is hungry—probably every two, two and a half, or three hours—is the best way of establishing a milk supply that will satisfy her hunger.[14] The law of supply and demand that you've probably heard about means that your supply of milk will increase as your child's appetite grows if you let your baby stimulate milk production by sucking.[15] Once the supply is established (at four to six weeks), you will be able to use an occasional supplementary bottle without affecting it greatly.

Building Up and Maintaining Your Milk Supply

The chances are excellent that you will have enough milk to feed your baby. Only a very small percentage of new mothers are physically incapable of nursing.[16] It is not unusual for newborn babies to want to nurse as often as every two or three hours during the day and perhaps twice at night. During the first two weeks of life a baby only takes an average of two or three ounces per feeding,[17] and, because breast milk is so easily digested, in an hour and a half the newborn's stomach is nearly empty again.[18] Nursing frequently is your baby's way of increasing milk production. If spending so much of your day nursing seems difficult or even overwhelming, try to remember that this pattern will not last for long. By the time your baby is a month or six weeks old, she will probably need fewer feedings. By then she will be getting an average of four or five ounces per feeding, and the nursing time itself will not be so long.[19]

If your nipples are sore, it helps to know that an infant gets most of the milk out of the breast in about five minutes of sucking. After eight minutes of nursing at each breast, very few babies get any more milk.[20] The rest of the sucking time is purely for enjoyment and to satisfy the baby's powerful need to suck. With only five or six minutes of nursing at each breast your baby will have received most of the nourishment she needs. If she still wants to suck, a pacifier or bottle of water or sugar water might help, but as soon as your nipples feel better, let her suck longer to keep up your milk supply. Nursing on both sides at each feeding and alternating the breast that is used first will also help maintain an ample supply of milk. When a breast has been emptied completely, your body then goes about producing enough milk to refill it.

Drink fluids and eat well. In order for your body to produce enough milk it is important that you drink a lot of fluids. Milk is particularly good, but fruit juices and even beer or wine in moderate amounts are also acceptable. For your own health and energy, it is also essential that you eat well; your need for plenty of high-protein foods is as great now as it was during pregnancy. Your doctor may also recommend continuing to take prenatal vitamins.

Get plenty of rest. To regain your strength and to produce plenty of milk it is important that you get enough rest.

Ideally you should take one morning and one afternoon nap each day throughout the first month. For the first three days after coming home from the hospital you really should do little else than stay in bed and nurse the baby. After that make a real effort to sleep whenever the baby does.[21] Use all the timesaving devices you can, and accept offers of help from friends and relatives. If for some reason you are unable to nap each day, be sure to lie down or put your feet up every time you nurse.

Relax at Feedings So Your Milk Will Let Down

Unless your milk is let down from the sacs where it is produced, your baby cannot get as much as she needs. Until this let-down occurs, the only milk available to the baby is the relatively small amount that is already in the larger ducts leading to your nipples.[22] The majority of milk comes out of the sacs, and the milk with the highest calorie content comes last. If your baby doesn't get this rich milk, she is apt to be hungry again sooner, and if your breasts are not emptied, they will not produce as much for the next feeding. Your baby will not be as full and as satisfied as she should be.[23]

The let-down reflex occurs when the let-down hormone (oxytocin) causes the cells around the sacs to contract, thereby squeezing the milk out into the larger milk ducts where your baby can get it by sucking.[24] Although ideally the reflex is set off automatically, it can be inhibited by fatigue, worry, fear, anxiety, and even embarrassment.[25] This is why you need to relax and rest at feedings. If you are having problems, there are ways of encouraging this reflex to occur whenever the baby is hungry.

Try to rest for a few minutes before each feeding. Eiger and Olds recommend stretching out and taking twenty deep breaths before nursing. Close your eyes and think about nothing, listen to soothing music, or do some light reading. Anything that helps you relax and take your mind off the problems of the day is appropriate.

Nurse in the same comfortable, quiet spot at each feeding.

Many new mothers choose a rocking chair; others nurse lying down for extra relaxation. Avoid being in the presence of critical relatives. Take the phone off the hook if it is likely to ring and distract you, or call a reassuring friend for comfort and enjoyment.

Take a drink of water, milk, juice, beer, or wine with *each* nursing session. (Alcoholic beverages, in small amounts, will have the added benefit of helping you unwind and forget about whatever may be worrying you at the time.) A relaxing drink before the early evening feeding may be especially helpful since you may have the least milk then.[26]

By associating a relaxing routine with letting down milk, you will be certain of having an adequate supply of nourishment for your baby. And having confidence that the milk is there will actually help to insure its continuation since you'll no longer be worrying about it. Once your let-down reflex is well established (probably by about a month after you begin nursing), this particular routine will not be quite so important. But don't forget the necessity of taking good care of yourself so that you will always know that you have plenty of milk. If at any time you are under stress, and you suspect that it may be affecting your let-down reflex, contact your doctor. The let-down hormone (oxytocin) is available as a nasal spray and in tablet form for these special circumstances.[27]

Each Baby Has a Different Nursing Style

Anyone who has seen a number of babies nurse notices the variety in their styles. This is a reflection of innate temperamental differences and is not caused by anything their mothers are doing. Any comprehensive book on breast-feeding will give you an amusing description of the various styles: Eager Beavers who nurse energetically, Slow Beginners who show little or no interest in nursing until perhaps the fourth or fifth day, Dawdlers and Sleepers who nurse for a while and then rest or fall asleep during feedings, and Excitable Nursers who get so wound up as they nurse that they lose the nipple and end up screaming in frustration.

As you become comfortable with your baby, you'll have ideas of how to help her nurse without frustration (for either of you). Handling Excitable Nursers quietly and calmly can make a big difference. Sleepers can be especially frustrating. Even though you know that in five minutes your baby can get most of the milk from your breast, it is discouraging when she falls asleep after nursing a few minutes on one side and then awakens only a short time later, screaming for food. Dr. Spock suggests that the digestive and nervous systems of a Sleeper may not yet be working well together. Having an ample supply of freely flowing milk may help to keep such babies interested in nursing, so it is important for the mother to be really relaxed at feeding times.[28] If your baby seems sleepy before a feeding, diaper her, play with her, or even let her cry for a short time until she becomes more alert. As time passes, this problem is likely to diminish.

TRY NOT TO GET DISCOURAGED

Do everything you can to make the conditions right for successful nursing, and then try to relax and enjoy feeding your baby. If your days simply don't seem to have enough hours for you to accomplish anything but breast-feeding, bear in mind that nursing is a special and relatively short-lived experience. As Karen Pryor points out, "The housework and the world's work will always be there; the nursing relationship is soon over. It is worth taking time off to enjoy it."[29] If you continue to feel overwhelmed by the time nursing takes, consider the possibility of changing your style slightly. (See "The Many Ways of Breast-feeding" in this chapter.) Don't panic every time you notice a change in yourself or in the baby. Both of you are still learning, and your body is adjusting to your baby's needs, which will necessarily vary from day to day or week to week. Breast-feeding can and will get easier as you go along, so don't let yourself get too discouraged. Try the suggestions contained in this chapter, and think positively.

Sore Nipples

Occasionally women develop sore nipples that really bother them throughout an entire feeding. Fair-skinned women seem to be more likely to have this problem. If it happens to you, don't wait until the pain becomes almost unbearable; take action right away.[30] Suggestions listed by Eiger and Olds include keeping your nipples dry (uncovered when possible), limiting sucking time to five minutes on the sore side, offering the less sore breast first, and changing your nursing position at each feeding (sitting, lying down, holding the baby in different ways, etc.).[31] If your nipple actually cracks and bleeds, do not offer that breast for twenty-four or forty-eight hours. Meanwhile, express milk by hand or by a rented electric breast pump, while your nipple heals, or try using a nipple shield. Then, resume feeding on that side gradually, continuing to express milk after the feeding to empty the breast.[32]

Plugged Ducts

Occasionally one or more of your milk ducts may become clogged so the milk cannot pass through them. If this happens, you are likely to find a small lump on one of your breasts that will probably be red and painful to the touch. Some doctors feel that a plugged duct can lead to a breast infection;[33] others disagree. Either way, it is important to take corrective measures. Eiger and Olds recommend the following ideas. Be sure your bra is not too tight. Put the baby in different positions at nursing time so that all the ducts are emptied. Check to see whether all the nipple openings are clear. If any are covered with dried secretions, wash them off gently. Offer the sore breast to the baby first so it will be emptied more completely.[34] Some women find that gently massaging the sore area toward the nipple helps to clear the duct. Putting a little lotion or powder on your breast before massaging it will minimize the irritation caused by rubbing.

Breast Infections (Mastitis)

Breast infections are most likely to develop during the first month but rarely occur before the end of the first week.[35] It is believed that bacteria from your baby's mouth enter the breast, probably through a tiny crack or abrasion in the nipple.[36] Infections often start with general aching and fever, much as if you were coming down with the flu. At about the same time you will probably discover that one part of your breast is hard, hot, red, and very tender.[37] Contact your doctor right away since prompt treatment can prevent the development of a more serious abcess.[38]

Breast infections are usually treated with modern drugs, and nursing need not be interrupted. In fact, more frequent nursing is one of the best ways of fighting the infection. Offer the sore breast first at every feeding. Try to stay in bed and get lots of rest. Placing a warm washcloth on the sore area for five to ten minutes at least once an hour should also bring some relief.[39] If medication is prescribed and you are worried about transmitting the drug to your baby through your milk, ask your doctor about that, too, or contact a member of La Leche League.

Six Weeks Is Often a Turning Point

By the time the baby is six weeks old, feedings are often shorter and less frequent.[40] You will be feeling stronger and will be able to get out more easily without getting so tired. If you feel like going out without the baby, do so; leave a bottle of formula (or a bottle of breast milk or water, if you prefer) with a sitter. As a new mother you have been working hard and you may want and need a change of scene. As a couple you need some time away from the baby. The hardest part of breast-feeding is probably behind you now; easier and more rewarding days will follow.[41] If you have been putting some of your own needs aside temporarily, this is a good time to work out a way to meet them while you are breast-feeding.

THE MANY WAYS OF BREAST-FEEDING

Methods of feeding are all too often described on an either-or basis: either you breast-feed totally, or you bottle feed. As helpful as some advocates of all-or-nothing breast-feeding are (such as La Leche League), their idea of motherhood may not suit you completely or may not fit at all. Perhaps you want to work, for example, or you have to work, and simply cannot be available for all feedings. Many mothers in this country and in other parts of the world succeed in combining their maternal and professional functions and get great satisfaction from both.[42] If your conception of parenthood includes sharing all aspects of baby care (including feedings) so that both parents can be free to pursue their desired goals, a combination of bottle and breast-feeding might meet your needs. Being away from your baby for one or two feedings a day—for whatever reason—may make exclusive breast-feeding difficult or impossible. But you don't have to give up breast-feeding altogether, or all at once.

Using Relief Bottles

Complete breast-feeding for the first four to six weeks has real advantages: it gives you a chance to establish an ample supply of milk, your let-down reflex will by then be functioning well, and your milk supply will have adjusted to the needs of your baby, so your breasts are less apt to become overfull and prone to plugged ducts or infections. But after the first month or so you may find it possible to add an occasional relief bottle to your nursing routine without adverse effects.[43] Some women find that daily supplementary bottles make their milk supply gradually decrease over a period of time until they have no more milk. Others are able to continue nursing indefinitely with only two or three feedings a day. Gradually losing your milk will allow you to wean your baby slowly and may prove to be a good way to work things out.

If you want to avoid losing your milk, you can manually express your own milk rather than using a supplementary formula.[44] Breast milk can be frozen for several months at zero degrees or for two weeks in the freezing compartment of a single-door refrigerator. It can be kept for forty-eight hours in the refrigerator.[45] Dr. Spock, La Leche League, and other breast-feeding books all explain how to express your milk. If you learn to express by hand to relieve engorgement in the first few weeks, you can also start then to offer the baby an occasional bottle of breast milk so she will get used to both kinds of nipples and will be less likely to refuse the bottle if and when you introduce it. Giving the baby an occasional bottle of water can help achieve this goal too.

Returning to Work While Breast-feeding

It is possible to return to work and still nurse, but trying to do both does pose problems. Support and perspective from mothers who have done it and the understanding of your own family may help you see how it can work out for you. If your job is flexible, obviously you'll have an easier time. But even if you are working eight hours a day away from your baby, you may find that nursing is still possible. Some full-time working mothers even feel it is the best arrangement, because they must relax to nurse their babies, even when they are tired, and otherwise they might not take the time to do this. They also can't neglect the physical contact with their babies that is so important for both mother and child. Nursing can be a surprisingly pleasant way to make the transition from work to family and can provide a guaranteed time of relaxation at the end of the day.[46]

You are more apt to discover a good way to combine nursing and work if you don't decide before you begin exactly how you want the experience to turn out. There are too many variables that you won't be able to consider fairly ahead of time. If you look at breast-feeding as a series of decisions to be made, initially during pregnancy, again when the baby is several weeks old, after the first couple of months, and so on, you can actively decide what is best as you go. Whatever decision you make at each point will be a good one if it takes into account your feelings and the needs of your situation. Any amount of nursing you do will have had benefits and hopefully pleasures.

Remember that the inevitable ups and downs of nursing may affect you more strongly if you are tired and on a tight schedule, as you inevitably will be some days. You will probably have days that are exhausting or discouraging when you will be tempted to give up nursing. When both you and the baby have a bad day, with the tension each of you feels being transmitted to the other, the situation may begin to seem impossible.

Before you decide to wean your baby, talk to a supportive friend or two. Sometimes just knowing other mothers have lived through such difficult and discouraging periods helps you get through them. Try to simplify your life if you can, and take a few days to think about weaning before you actively begin.

Take things one step at a time and have the confidence that whatever your decision at each stage, you have made the best possible choice for your own situation. If you avoid using other people's standards for success, and support each other as a family in the arrangements you decide to make, you will all profit from the breast-feeding experience, regardless of how long it lasts.

Suggestions for working mothers. If you wish to continue giving your baby nothing but breast milk after returning to work, you could try nursing in the morning, as soon as you return home in the evening, and around 10 P.M. (if your baby still takes a feeding at that time). You can then express milk into a jar during your lunch break and refrigerate it. The next day it can be used for a midday feeding from a cup or bottle. This will relieve the pressure in your breasts and stimulate your milk supply so you'll continue to have enough milk for your baby.[47]

Some working mothers find it possible to nurse their babies during their lunch hours or afternoon coffee breaks. Other women take their infants with them to their place of work for a couple of months, until such an arrangement becomes impractical. Adding a couple of formula feedings in the middle of the day is another alternative. Although doing so will decrease your milk supply, it can be a comfortable and satisfactory way of gradually weaning your baby without a sudden break in your style of mothering.

WEANING

Weaning can occur any time from soon after the birth until several years later. Karen Pryor reports that some breast-fed babies wean themselves around the age of nine months;[48] others are eager to continue nursing indefinitely. You may be ready to wean your baby before she naturally weans herself. The reasons women have for weaning their babies are as varied as their individual circumstances. One generalization that seems to apply in many cases, however, is that making the decision is difficult. One day you feel quite convinced that using a bottle or a cup would be much more satisfactory, all things considered; the next day you wonder whether giving up nursing is really best and you are afraid you might later regret it.

As you consider weaning, it sometimes helps to remember that even if you have been breast-feeding for only a few weeks, you have probably already given your baby some protection against infection. Nursing for six weeks will have helped your body return to normal more quickly. Weaning at whatever point, as long as you have thought it through and feel that it is the right decision for all of you, should leave you with no lasting feelings of guilt or uneasiness. While it is natural that you will have some doubts and even some moments of anguish, don't let anyone upset you once you have made up your mind. Unhelpful comments from friends and relatives must be ignored.

You and your husband are the only people who can fully understand the pressures that bear on you and the feelings you have about what is best in your particular situation. Some couples reach a point where they feel pulled apart by the exclusiveness of breast-feeding. The husband may continue to feel resentful of the demands it makes on his wife. Both of you may feel you need more time together but relief bottles are for some reason not a solution. Or a woman finds it impossible to leave her baby but feels tied down and is beginning to feel resentful. Maybe minor annoyances, like leaking milk and sore breasts, have continued much longer than you expected and are really beginning to bother you and keep you from feeling you have recovered completely. Or you may be resuming a number of your former activities or going back to work, and are beginning to feel that nursing is more of a duty than a pleasure, especially when you are tired. Whatever your reasons, if breast-feeding seems more than you can handle and you feel quite certain that bottle feeding will ease the pressures on you, have the courage to stop nursing. The method of feeding that turns out to be the most satisfying for you is going to be the best for your whole family, including your baby.

When you do decide to wean, be sure to do it as gradually as possible. Begin by decreasing your intake of fluids somewhat, so your body will produce less milk. Then, depending on your baby's age and sucking needs, offer a bottle or a cup at one feeding (preferably the feeding in which your baby shows the least interest). Continue in this manner at a pace that is comfortable for you until the baby is weaned and your body is producing virtually no milk.[49] If you begin to have doubts, you can slow the weaning process down, or if you feel strongly about weaning, you can be persistent in carrying it out. A gradual approach is much easier on your body and on your baby than abruptly stopping all breast-feeding. If you continue to feed her in a relaxed and comfortable way (now using a bottle or cup), both of you will adjust well. Don't suddenly stop holding a young baby during feedings; infants continue to need warmth and close contact with their parents.

You will probably notice some physical changes after you stop breast-feeding. Hormonal readjustment will occur until your body has reached the balance it had before you became pregnant. Don't be surprised if it takes several months for your breasts to lose all their milk.[50] If you haven't begun menstruating, you will soon begin again. Some women have problems with their hair falling out; this is temporary, and you won't lose it all! If you had a tendency toward oily skin and scalp before you became pregnant, it may return.

Emotional reactions to weaning are also normal. Depending

on your particular circumstances, you may feel uneasy, a bit anxious, and possibly somewhat guilty. Some women feel a need to bring their sense of mothering back into focus once this important aspect of their relationship with the baby has come to an end. These feelings usually pass as you see how well you and your baby manage with the greater independence you have. Now you can turn your attention to the next stage of your baby's life and continue exploring the possibilities of closeness and independence you both need for growing.

RECOMMENDED READING

Eiger, Marvin S., and Olds, Sally Wendkos. *The Complete Book of Breastfeeding.* New York: Bantam, in arrangement with Workman, 1972.

An excellent source of information, this book is a relatively open-minded presentation of breast-feeding. It recognizes that mothers may want or have to work and acknowledges the occasional usefulness of a relief bottle of formula. It includes interesting information about "sex and the nursing mother" and a separate chapter addressed to the father. Several pages are devoted to a discussion of postpartum blues and several to feelings about weaning.

Gerard, Alice. *Please Breast Feed Your Baby.* New York: New American Library, Signet, 1970.

Although short in comparison to the other two guides, this book is straightforward and relatively unbiased in its presentation of the basics of breast-feeding. While it probably contains enough information for the woman who has no major difficulties, it lacks the detailed suggestions that the other books contain. Gerard fails to consider the uneasy feelings a new mother may have, nor does she discuss the father's role very much. She does, however, acknowledge the value of an occasional relief bottle and is open-minded about weaning.

Pryor, Karen. *Nursing Your Baby.* New York: Pocket Books, 1973.

Karen Pryor's book contains a great deal of useful information regarding milk production, let-down, and possible complications that may develop with breast-feeding. She cautions the nursing mother about expecting instant success, but assures her that by following her recommendations for establishing and maintaining a good milk supply she will find nursing an extremely rewarding experience.

Pryor is supportive of the nursing mother, but in describing the closeness of the "nursing couple" (mother and baby) she fails to acknowledge the range of feelings that the father might have, or the need of a husband and wife to maintain a life apart from their baby. Her views on mothers working and relief bottles may seem out of date to some parents. Nonetheless the book can be very helpful and encouraging.

5

Re-establishing Closeness as a Couple

What [new parents] really need to learn is how to adapt themselves to changed roles vis à vis each other and how to acquire the capacity of enjoying each transitional phase of their life together. For the whole of marriage is really a series of transitions, in which the identity of each partner is transmuted by processes involving the birth and development of children, the new stresses involved in changing relationships in the family, and the daily battles and satisfactions and pleasures of living together. Each marriage has a life of its own and is as alive and growing as a tree.[1]

Sheila Kitzinger

WHAT ABOUT YOUR LIFE AS A COUPLE?

Although there are now three of you instead of only two, your life as a couple continues to be of special importance. Your ability to accept and take pleasure in each other will set the tone of your family. In spite of your excitement about the baby, there will be times when all the attention focused on her keeps you apart. Having children makes marriage less spontaneous and exciting in some ways, and it often takes more effort than you expect to get back together comfortably. If you can express any disappointment or resentment you have about the baby coming between you, you will be able to put more of your energy into re-establishing closeness as a couple.

The important point is that the fears you may have about your life as a couple can become the starting point for developing an awareness and an aliveness that will strengthen your relationship. For this to happen, you'll have to give top priority in the time you spend together to sharing your feelings and doing things that you both enjoy.

Tense Times

It is difficult to feel close when the atmosphere in the house is tense and many of your former pleasures seem to be lost in the chaos and confusion of meeting basic needs. The times when you are together—around dinner and in the evening—may be when you are both worn out. The amount of work still to be done can be discouraging; very possibly dinner isn't ready and everyone is hungry and short-tempered. You may want to sit down and talk with each other, but neither may feel up to an account of the other's day or capable of being friendly for very long. Nonetheless you may strongly feel the need to communicate in some way.

It isn't surprising if both of you have mixed feelings about how to get in touch with each other. The times you feel like being close may be times when the baby demands attention. Making love in the morning, for example, may no longer be possible. There is no such thing as intimacy when a baby—your baby—is screaming in the background. If she sleeps late, one of you may have been up with her two or three times during the night and feel too tired to respond. And even if you plan a time to relax together, the tension can build up to a point where it is difficult to unwind.

There are no easy answers, but it helps to realize that the baby's needs do become more predictable, and you won't feel so exhausted as you adjust to the new demands on your life. Think of ways to reduce the tension when you are together. For example, if the time around dinner does cause problems, a quick snack might improve the situation. Even if dinner is late, at least you won't be irritable and starved. If you want some time together before dinner, try to ease the baby's schedule (if she has any) so that she is asleep then, or feed her just before the homecoming chaos if you think that will help. Split up the work so you'll both soon be able to relax. If your baby sleeps during the early evening hours, make a point of spending that time together, doing something you both enjoy. A quiet dinner might lift your spirits. Or, if the baby is awake then, you may be able to find an activity that provides temporary amusement—a baby swing, mobile, or special toy, perhaps. As the weeks go by, you will discover your own special ways of getting through the rough periods more easily.

Having Fun Together

Talking over feelings and attitudes about your baby, about being parents, and about the kind of family you want to become is vital to your relationship: you need to know your partner cares about your feelings even if they are confused. But when you are not making sense, it's important to help each other see that you have talked enough and that you need to relate in other ways—touching, laughing, doing things you like together.

At first you may want to stay home and read the paper, watch television, or invite some friends over. You may both feel that you can have as much fun with the baby, either at home or by going out as a family. But taking the baby along will eventually limit your life as a couple: you'll lose touch with some important parts of your relationship. You need to do whatever you enjoy most, eating out, going to movies or concerts, swimming, visiting with friends of all ages. Don't push each other into leaving your baby before you are ready, but don't let too many months go by before you try an evening out; you may forget how good it feels. The core of enjoyment and the sense of possibility in your life together can keep your family full of hope and flexibility.

Finding Time Together at Home

Practically speaking, you can't always be off by yourselves, and you wouldn't always want to be. You'll find new ways of having fun together at home too. Eating a late dinner occasionally after the baby is asleep or a late brunch on the weekend while the baby takes a morning nap can be a welcome change. Choose a recipe and have fun concocting it together. Then, even if the baby wakes up just as you sit down to eat, at least you will have enjoyed preparing the meal. And if it turns out to be the best food you have ever tasted, you both will have been responsible!

You might enjoy reading books aloud—it's a great time to

discover the good children's books you may want to read to your baby later on; by then some of them will seem like old favorites. Think back to the books you were fond of as a child and try to find them at the library. You'll have fun and may find out more about each other's childhood.

Other possibilities are as broad as your imagination—from taking a shower together or washing each other's hair, to planting a garden, indoors or out. Do some dancing, develop your interest in music, play your favorite games, or set up a badminton net in the yard. Give some thought, too, to special ways of unwinding at the end of an exhausting day so you can focus on each other instead of on daily frustrations.

RESUMING A FULL SEX LIFE

Expressing your love for each other in a physical way is as important now as it ever was. But waiting until the woman's episiotomy has healed may seem like waiting forever, and it can be very discouraging for both of you. If you have already begun making time to be together, you have overcome one of the greatest obstacles. But you also need to find ways of meeting your sexual needs before actual intercourse is possible. You can begin by relaxing together and being open about what you want. Either of you can help the other reach orgasm even if you aren't ready for vaginal intercourse. Or if one of you is still uneasy about orgasm, you need to feel free to say so. You each have sexual needs; it's just a question of making the effort to say what they are so you can find ways to meet them.

"Pleasuring"

"Pleasuring" is the term Masters and Johnson use to describe thinking and feeling sensuously with each other without any pressure to proceed to intercourse. Some couples have done this before, some haven't. Try to discover how many ways you can be close—stroking, smelling, exploring with your eyes and hands, or smoothing lotion over each other's bodies.[2] Learning your own ways of "pleasuring" each other may help you communicate your needs; if one or both of you wants to go on to reach orgasm, you obviously can. If the idea is new to you, it may seem awkward at first, but your caring will help it become the basis of a new closeness.

Resuming Sexual Intercourse

If you are uneasy about resuming intercourse, it may partly be because you aren't sure what to expect. Doctors often neglect to tell their patients about problems that may arise, and even friends who have been through the experience hesitate to talk about it. Intercourse after childbirth is different for each couple, but there are common problems. Most doctors would probably agree that the six-week period they usually suggest for refraining from intercourse is somewhat arbitrary and really for their own convenience. They would like to see the woman first to be sure she has healed well and her cervix is returning to its normal size. Women should feel free to request an earlier appointment or simply ask about having intercourse before the postpartum checkup. Some women feel ready as early as three weeks after the delivery and some don't. It depends partly on how quickly the incision heals and what complications there might have been. If intercourse is comfortable for a woman, it probably isn't harmful. But if either of you is hesitant, ask your doctor for an opinion.

There are other factors to consider. A woman sometimes feels under pressure to begin having intercourse as soon as possible because whether or not she feels ready, she is sure her husband is. Sometimes, on the other hand, the man feels hesitant (perhaps because he is afraid of hurting his wife or unsure of what to expect), and the woman is the one who is eager to begin. How much your baby sleeps and cries, how much help you have had with the work around the house, and how tired you are will also influence your feelings. If you have found ways to be intimate already, you won't need to pressure each other. It really helps if you can accept what the other can give and let things evolve naturally. Both of you may recognize some of the feelings expressed by a woman in Carl Rogers's *Becoming Partners:*

I'm thinking about when you feel like making love and I don't
—usually that is a Bad Scene. I am closed—tight—and that
makes me feel awful. How could I possibly give anything when
I feel like that? Then one day I got a glimpse of something new
—I didn't feel like making love but I was really caring about you
—wanting to make you feel good. I lit some candles and put on
a record we both like. I said, "roll over" and I gave you a
fantastic back rub—pounding, caressing, letting my long hair
trail over your bare back. I put my cheek on your back—my
nose, my ear, my lips. I rubbed the tight muscles at the base of
your neck. I traced a pattern there. . . . It makes sense that you
would rather have a back rub freely and joyfully given than
make love to a body without a soul in it. I must admit, a cup of
hot tea (with honey and lemon even) won't always satisfy a man
who wants to make love. But a funny thing happens, sometimes,
when I am free to give what I want to give at the moment—it
opens me up, makes me feel like a human being again—and
who knows what might happen then?[3]

Common Problems with Intercourse

For some couples, intercourse after childbirth causes no
problems at all. Most of the problems that do commonly occur
are not difficult to deal with, once you know how. Don't assume you will get all the information you need from your
doctor; many neglect to volunteer some of the most helpful
suggestions, possibly because they are afraid that mentioning
difficulties will create them. But many couples with minor
problems never benefit from simple advice that might help
them make a good start in their sex life. Whether you are using
a birth control method that is new to you or your former
method, see the end of this chapter for information about
possible complications you may be unaware of.

Lubrication. There is a chance that a woman's vagina will not
lubricate as easily or as much as before (especially if she is
nursing) because of the state of her hormones and genitals
after childbirth.[4] If you have never before experienced problems with lubrication, both of you might be alarmed by the
discomfort you feel. Some describe it as a "tightness" felt by
both partners. To others it feels as though there is some obstacle in the vagina. If the pain is in a particular spot, it probably

is related to the episiotomy; there may be a little lump of scar tissue which is especially tender. If the discomfort is generalized, it may be caused by insufficient lubrication or perhaps by the temporary tightness of the vaginal opening and the tenseness the woman may still feel about this part of her body.

Using a lubricant is easy; it can become part of your lovemaking if you put it on each other. If the man gently applies the lubricant in and around the vagina, he will have a better idea of where the sensitive places are. Keep in mind that putting cold lubricant on an erect penis takes some skill and may hinder the erection. If the coolness of the jelly bothers you, then put it on in advance of making love. Use whatever amount feels comfortable. Lubricating jellies, such as K-Y, are soothing, water soluble, and relatively tasteless and odorless. If the idea appeals to you, your own saliva may work as well.

Women who are experiencing problems with lubrication (especially if they are nursing) should ask their doctor about vaginal estrogen creams. These may help increase natural lubrication so that no additional lubricant is needed. The problem of vaginal lubrication usually clears up when ovulation begins again, which for mothers who are not nursing usually occurs within two months of delivery. It is difficult to predict when women who are breast-feeding will ovulate—possibly within several months, perhaps after they stop nursing exclusively and begin to add solid foods to the baby's diet, or maybe not until after the baby is completely weaned.

For some couples problems with intercourse seem to drag on for weeks or even months. Why does this happen? There can be physical reasons for a woman's discomfort, and doctors may be able to explain or correct them. For example, Masters and Johnson report that deep pain in the pelvis can be caused by tears in the ligaments which support the uterus, and it is possible (though not common) for such tears to be caused during childbirth.[5]

More likely is the possibility that your minor problems are being aggravated by the way you feel about having intercourse. If you are tense because of continual difficulties, or are trying to be careful because the woman feels pain or because you are worried that the baby might wake up and interrupt lovemaking, understandably it is hard to become really involved with each other. The less involved you both are, the less the woman will lubricate. It may help both of you if you realize that the secretion of lubricating material in the vagina is the response that corresponds to a man's erection. Until she begins lubricating (even if her lubrication has decreased in the postpartum period), a woman is not ready either physically or psychologically for intercourse.[6] Be aware that it may take a little longer than it used to before the woman is ready for penetration: Masters and Johnson have found that women in the first two months postpartum are slower to respond to sexual stimulation and respond less intensively physically although intercourse doesn't necessarily seem less satisfying to them for that reason.[7]

Whether your problem is one of lubrication, pain, or difficulty becoming involved, try to talk about your feelings and overcome your hesitations. The two of you may be uneasy about using a lubricant, for example, hoping lubrication will not be a problem. This may just increase tension about intercourse and make you both begin to avoid intimacy. Overcoming the feeling that a lubricant is not natural or should not be necessary can do much to help your situation—you'll both be more comfortable, relaxed, and involved. Take your time, and enjoy being close. Be confident that you can respond to each other fully even though there are problems.

Finding a comfortable position. To minimize discomfort related to the episiotomy, try varying your positions for intercourse. Women with an incision that goes off to one side say it is helpful if their partner leans to the opposite side. Most episiotomies are midline (right down the middle, toward the rectum). Choose a position in which the penis presses against the front part of the vagina and the clitoris, rather than the tender area in back[8]—a side, woman-on-top, or man-behind-the-woman position, for example. It helps if the woman guides the man's penis into her, relaxing as much as possible. Occasionally a woman feels as if her vagina needs to be stretched a bit.

Doctors sometimes suggest that lubricating well and then inserting a couple of fingers helps this stretching process when necessary. Remember that if a woman is nursing, her breasts may be sore, especially when they are full of milk. This might be another reason to vary positions.

Fatigue. It is hard to enjoy sex when you feel like collapsing and sleeping forever, but you both need the closeness of making love to revitalize you. Being parents takes a lot of energy at first, no matter how you are sharing work at home and away from home. Cooperating with each other and with other parents in similar situations (baby-sitting, potluck suppers, sharing ideas and feelings) can be helpful. If you are able to stay in close touch with each other physically and emotionally, you may be able to figure out ways of limiting the work load and getting more rest. It just doesn't make sense for either of you to be under such stress that you begin living mechanically or without any time to enjoy life and each other.

Nursing and Sexuality

Nursing can add complications to your sex life. Some women do not respond to breast stimulation while they are nursing, for example. This may not make any difference to you as a couple, or it may cause feelings of conflict or resentment in one or both of you. Some women let down so much milk when/sexually stimulated that you both get soaked. One solution is to wear a bra and nursing pads that provide enough pressure to stop the flow of milk or at least absorb it, but wearing a bra may seem less than romantic. Another possibility is to nurse the baby shortly before lovemaking. With less milk, the problem of leaking diminishes, and, with a full stomach, your baby is apt to sleep soundly. It may help to remember that your let-down reflex is part of your larger sense of relaxation, pleasure, and involvement in lovemaking. Some women spout milk as soon as they become sexually aroused. For others, milk flow coincides with orgasm. Seeing the problem as part of a pleasurable process may help you enjoy it, or at least make it easier for you to accept it.

There seem to be conflicting reports on the effect of nursing on interest in sex. Some women notice a lack of interest in intercourse while breast-feeding their babies. In *Nursing Your Baby*, Karen Pryor suggests that this might be due in part to lactation hormones. She points out that nursing mothers often don't have the mood swings and peaks of desire usually associated with their menstrual cycle. She adds that lack of desire may also be due to the closeness, the feeling of being admired, and the reassurance of being needed and wanted that nursing a baby provides.[9] On the other hand, Masters and Johnson report the opposite. Their group of nursing mothers, as compared with non-nursing mothers, showed a higher level of sexual interest during the first three months after delivery. Some reported that nursing itself produced sexual stimulation, and as a group they described being interested in resuming intercourse as soon as possible.[10]

Whether nursing makes a woman eager for intercourse or hesitant about it, if you are close as a couple there are other equally important pulls towards intimacy and intercourse. Even if nursing affects the way a woman feels sexually, it will probably not stand in the way of her sharing a full sex life.

Nostalgia for the Way Things Were

Although some new parents express added satisfaction from lovemaking after childbirth, if you are faced with problems relating to intercourse, you may begin to think about how simple and satisfying sex used to be. It may at times seem easier to turn all your attention toward the baby instead of re-establishing intimacy with each other. At this point you may give up without openly admitting it. You simply try less and less often to make love or to solve the problems that are preventing you from making a good sexual adjustment.

Rather than letting yourselves fall into such a destructive pattern, begin now to deal with the problems creatively. In the midst of other changes in your life it is vital that you feel that the sexual aspect of your relationship is going well. Try not to feel that intimacy must always lead to intercourse and discover the enjoyment of "pleasuring" each other with or without orgasm. Try to keep your sense of humor and be supportive of each other's efforts. Your commitment to accept each other as you are now, rather than nostalgia about how much easier or better things used to be, will help you move ahead.

Be sure to keep the lines of communication open between the two of you. Share your anxieties, not only about sex, but about other aspects of your new life as well. But help each other know when talking is getting nowhere and you need to relax. Be gentle with each other's feelings. When things aren't going well, admit your fears and uneasiness and then work together toward finding a solution. Remember that you are not alone in these problems—many other new parents share them.

If you've tried everything and nothing seems to help, you might find it useful to read Masters and Johnson or consider going together to a doctor or counselor. Try to find someone who is known for being helpful in matters related to sexuality. Describe your difficulties and ask for suggestions. Don't be put off by being told that it "sounds psychological." Masters and Johnson have made it clear that in sexuality there is often a fine line between the physical and the psychological. Regardless of the cause, which is probably not one but several factors combined, what you need are solutions. Problems like these are common and solutions do exist, so don't give up until you find one.

RE-EVALUATING YOUR METHOD OF BIRTH CONTROL

For the past nine months or more you probably haven't given any thought to contraception. Now you need to think about it again unless you are prepared for the possibility of another pregnancy. This is a good time for the two of you to re-evaluate your method of contraception, whatever it may have been, remembering that a woman's body changes after she has given birth to a baby. This section may offer some new information you will want to consider. Although it attempts to include the latest thinking on various methods, this discussion will soon be outdated by new findings, especially about IUDs and birth control pills. You should find out what additional information is available at the time you are making your decision so that you will be as fully aware as possible of new factors that may affect you.

To save money on birth control devices, consider going to a Planned Parenthood clinic, a women's free clinic, or a Department of Health family planning clinic. Condoms are sometimes free, and other methods cost considerably less or may be free in limited supply. The examination which accompanies the prescription for pills, IUDs, and diaphragms will also cost less. Be sure to find out how long records are kept by the clinic in case you need them at a later date, especially if any problems should develop.

Pills

For women who are not nursing, birth control pills remain the most effective means of contraception (besides male or female sterilization) if they are taken regularly. As you may know, pills work by providing the body with synthetic hormones which prevent ovulation from occurring and cause local changes in the uterus that would make pregnancy impossible even if an egg should be released.[11] Women have different reactions to the many brands of pills on the market, but in general those with the lowest doses of estrogen (the low-dose pills currently have 0.05 mg. of estrogen) produce the fewest side effects and complications. The combination pills may be safer than sequential pills because they have less estrogen and because each pill contains both estrogen and progesterone. These combined hormones tend to balance each other's effects in a woman's body.[12] *Women who are breast-feeding should not take the pill.* Pills can reduce the quantity and food value of breast milk, and some of the hormones are secreted in the milk and absorbed by the baby.[13]

Before prescribing birth control pills, doctors should do a thorough medical history of the woman who wants them. There are unanswered questions about the relationship between the pill and certain diseases and disorders: women who have ever had blood clots, for example, who currently have vaginal bleeding of unknown cause, as well as those who have breast cancer or serious disturbances in liver functions, are advised not to use pills. Doctors will also want to know about other problems like migraine headaches, diabetes, epilepsy, hepatitis, mental illness, high blood pressure, or a family history of breast or genital cancer.[14]

Since the safety of taking birth control pills is not completely established, it is important that a woman taking them report any changes in her body or general health to her doctor. Early warning signs of blood clots in legs include pain, redness, or swelling.[15] Blurring of vision, continuing headaches, nervousness, or depression indicate a need for immediate medical attention and should not be ignored. Most women experience no difficulties whatsoever; those who do should report them promptly.

Advantages of pills. They are easy and effective, provided they are taken as directed. They tend to regulate and lighten menstrual flow and may also eliminate cramps and premenstrual tension. They in no way interfere with the spontaneity of intercourse.

Disadvantages. The cost of pills tends to be fairly high—from $2.00 to $3.00 for a month's supply. Remembering to take the pill every day may be a problem. Women with previously irregular menstrual cycles who take pills sometimes find that on discontinuing them, they fail to ovulate regularly, at least for the first several months.

Some women notice annoying side effects while taking the pill, and in some cases a brand of pills that was satisfactory before pregnancy causes problems after childbirth. Among the complaints listed are nausea, fatigue, breast soreness, weight gain or loss, nervousness, depression, headaches, spotting between periods, or an increased susceptibility to vaginal infections. (Reports on the connection between the pill and a woman's susceptibility to vaginal infections conflict.) Some women notice a decrease in sexual desire and a lessening of vaginal lubrication; others find that menstrual flow completely disappears.[16] If these side effects don't diminish or disappear by the third month on pills, check with your doctor. Sometimes a different brand has less noticeable side effects, or none that you find bothersome.

IUDs

The next most effective method of contraception for women whose bodies will tolerate it is the IUD (intrauterine device). Having a baby increases a woman's chances of successfully using such a device. IUDs are generally made of malleable plastic—some with fine copper wire attached—and are inserted into the uterus by a special applicator. The shape and kind of IUD that is most suitable depends partly on the size and position of a woman's uterus and partly on whether or not she has had children. Two kinds that are often recommended for women who have had one or two children are the Lippes loop[17] and the new Cu 7, which has recently been approved for use by the Food and Drug Administration. Copper IUDs (Cu 7) need to be replaced every two or three years because the copper gradually dissolves (with no harmful effect on the woman's body, apparently) and eventually makes the device ineffective.[18]

There are various theories on how the IUD is able to prevent pregnancy. One is that the presence of the device in the uterus causes chemical changes that keep the sperm from fertilizing the egg.[19] Another suggests that the device may prevent an already fertilized egg from attaching itself to the uterine wall.[20] Still another claims that IUDs may stimulate the entry of many white blood cells into the uterus which attack and possibly destroy fertilized eggs. Copper IUDs interfere with fertilization and implantation, and dissolved copper is poisonous to human sperm.[21] For the latest information regarding side effects, effectiveness, and how IUDs work, check with a doctor or other sources such as Planned Parenthood, women's free clinics, or Department of Health family planning clinics.

The IUD is inserted in the uterus through a sterile plastic tube. The procedure tends to be less painful after childbirth than before the uterus has been stretched by pregnancy, but

some women do experience considerable pain, much like contractions in labor or strong menstrual cramps. It is unwise for
a woman to go alone to the doctor's office or clinic because if
she feels weak or faint afterwards, she will need help getting
home. Some doctors anesthetize the cervix or give pain pills;
others simply ask their patients to relax and breathe deeply.
Doctors usually insert the IUD during or right after a menstrual period when the cervix is a bit softer and more open,
and there is no possibility of pregnancy. Women who are
nursing and not menstruating should ask their doctor's advice
on insertion; usually at least a six-week wait after childbirth is
recommended so that the uterus can return to normal.[22]

Advantages of the IUD. Women who are able to use IUDs are
usually very enthusiastic about them. While the initial expense
of having the IUD inserted may be fairly high (often $25.00 to
$50.00 for insertion and a follow-up visit with a private doctor,
less at a clinic), there are no expenses thereafter for contraception. Once inserted, no more thought needs to be given to
contraception, except to make sure that the IUD is in place.
During the first three months the nylon threads that can be felt
hanging from the cervix should be checked frequently (ideally
before having intercourse); after that time, checking after
menstrual periods is probably adequate. If you are unable to
find the threads by inserting a finger into the vagina, or if you
feel plastic protruding from the cervix, have the IUD checked
to be sure it is still in place.

Disadvantages. Some women cannot tolerate the IUD and
experience either immediate or delayed pain, often followed
by expulsion. Many women experience minor discomfort and
heavy bleeding while adjusting to the IUD, but these problems
diminish after the first several weeks. Occasionally heavy menstrual bleeding continues to be a problem, and although it is
not usually dangerous, it should be reported to the doctor.[23]
The copper devices may create fewer difficulties of this sort
than other IUDs. At the time when an IUD is inserted, there
is a slight risk of pelvic infection. It is important that a woman

be free from any infection when she makes an appointment to have the device put in.[24] There is a very slight possibility (1 out of 2500) of uterine perforation by the IUD either at the time of insertion or by contractions which may push the IUD through the wall of the uterus.[25] If the threads cannot be located, an X ray will reveal whether the IUD has in fact gone through into the abdominal cavity. If it has, the device can be removed surgically.[26]

For the first few months, some doctors recommend using a second contraceptive (such as foam) each time you have intercourse;[27] expulsion of the IUD is most likely during this time, and it can happen without being noticed. Once a woman has successfully used an IUD for three months, the likelihood of expulsion is greatly reduced.[28] To be absolutely sure of avoiding pregnancy, one of you may want to use an additional contraceptive during the time the woman is ovulating. Recently, higher-than-expected pregnancy rates and pregnancy complications with IUDs have come to light. A woman who gets pregnant with an IUD in place should check with her doctor right away and have it removed once pregnancy has been confirmed. The risk to both mother and baby of continuing a pregnancy with an IUD in the uterus may be greater than it was first thought to be. IUDs have not been regulated (except those with copper) by the federal government because they are considered devices rather than drugs; this may change because of findings in the last year about potential dangers and complications of intrauterine devices.

Diaphragms

The third most effective method of birth control is the diaphragm, a round rubber device which, when inserted into the vagina, surrounds the cervix and thereby prevents sperm from getting into the uterus. It is important that a diaphragm fit well. A woman's size should be checked for possible change after childbirth, miscarriage, or if she gains or loses more than ten pounds.[29] When a woman is first fitted with a diaphragm, she should learn how to insert it. The doctor or nurse can demonstrate how, and then give the woman several chances to try it so she is confident that she has the right technique.

Properly placed, the front rim of the diaphragm fits snugly behind the pubic bone, the round dome covers the cervix, and the far rim rises behind the cervix. To remove the device, the fingers should be hooked under the front rim (by the pubic bone) and the diaphragm pulled down and out.

Advantages of the diaphragm. The diaphragm is completely safe to use; that is, it has no side effects or health hazards associated with it. Though it is less effective than the pill or an IUD, its failure rate can be reduced considerably by using it carefully, with ample spermicidal jelly or cream (about one teaspoon) on one or both sides of the diaphragm and around the rim. (Authorities differ on this point;[30] if cream on the rim makes it difficult to insert, don't put it there.) Some couples find that they can share insertion and enjoy it as part of sexual foreplay.

Disadvantages. Although the diaphragm itself costs only about $4.50, if you include the appointment for fitting ($15.00 or more for a private doctor, less in a clinic) and the tubes of spermicidal cream or jelly you must continue to buy ($2.00 to $3.00), the cost does add up. Since the diaphragm must be inserted before intercourse, some couples find it inconvenient. To work effectively it should be inserted no more than two hours before intercourse and should remain in place for at least six hours after ejaculation.[31] If you want to have intercourse a second time (before the six hours have elapsed), insert another teaspoon of jelly or cream with an applicator into the vagina beforehand (without removing the diaphragm), or use foam.[32] It can be left in place for as long as twenty-four hours, after which time it should be washed with mild soap and dried.[33] Be sure to check for leaks by filling the diaphragm with water and by holding it up to the light to check for weak spots. Diaphragms sometimes become dislodged during intercourse, which is a further disadvantage, and certain jellies or creams prove irritating to some women or men. If either of you finds this to be the case, try another brand. Women who are allergic to rubber can get plastic diaphragms.

Condoms

The condom is a thin rubber or animal-tissue sheath worn by the man on his erect penis during intercourse. If used carefully, it can be almost as effective as the diaphragm in keeping the sperm from entering the uterus. Reservoir-tip condoms provide room for the semen at the end. If not using this kind, be sure to leave a half-inch of space at the tip when putting the condom on. To use a condom effectively, the penis must be withdrawn from the vagina while still erect; otherwise the sperm can easily escape. Used in combination with foam, condoms are considered nearly as effective as birth control pills.[34]

Advantages of condoms. Condoms are easily purchased at drugstores and have no side effects or health hazards associated with their use. They can help prevent the spreading of genital infections a man or woman might have.[35] Some women appreciate the fact that the man is taking some or all of the responsibility for contraception by using a condom. You both may enjoy putting the condom on the man's penis when making love.

Disadvantages. The cost of condoms is fairly high ($.30 to $.50 each). Some couples object to having to interrupt foreplay to put on the condom or feel they must be too careful using it to enjoy relaxed intercourse. If vaginal lubrication is scant, it helps to get lubricated condoms, but you'll need to be especially careful since they tend to slip. Or apply some spermicidal cream or jelly, or a lubricating jelly to the condom (already in place) to make entry more comfortable and to keep it from tearing during intercourse. Do not use Vaseline or other oils as they can cause the rubber to deteriorate. It is important to hold the ring at the top of the condom as the man withdraws in order to keep semen from spilling and possibly entering the vagina. If this happens, the woman should immediately insert an applicator of spermicidal cream, jelly, or foam into her vagina.

Foams

Foam is an aerosol cream containing a spermicidal agent. It is released into the vagina through a special applicator. Even if inserted properly so as to provide a barrier to the cervix and uterus, foam is the least reliable contraceptive discussed so far. Its effectiveness can be increased somewhat by using two applications each time and by using it immediately before intercourse. Shake the can well—the more bubbles the foam has, the better it blocks the sperm.[36] Foam should be applied no more than fifteen minutes before intercourse;[37] any longer than that will decrease its effectiveness. In combination with the condom, foam is nearly as reliable as birth control pills.[38] Some doctors consider foam adequate protection for women who are breast-feeding, at least for the first couple of months after childbirth.

Advantages of foam. It is relatively inexpensive, a little more than $3.00 for a medium-sized can. There are no side effects or health hazards associated with the use of foam, and some women find it much easier to insert than a diaphragm. It also adds lubrication which can be helpful in the weeks following childbirth. It is easily available and quick to apply.

Disadvantages. Since foam is only effective for a short time, some couples find it annoying to have to interrupt foreplay to apply it, or find that the time limit interferes with their spontaneity. Some women or men are irritated by foam; it can sting or burn. If this happens, change to another brand. Foam must be left in for six to eight hours following intercourse, and douching during this time is not advisable.[39] Always keep an extra container of foam on hand since it may be difficult to tell when the can is almost empty.

Unreliable Contraceptive Measures

Using douches, vaginal suppositories, or spermicidal creams and jellies (not in combination with the diaphragm or condom) to prevent conception may be better than nothing, but they are not reliable methods of birth control. Neither is withdrawal of the penis before ejaculating since some of the semen is likely to get into the vagina anyway.[40] The rhythm method of avoiding pregnancy (having intercourse only during the woman's "safe period") also has its difficulties, particularly if the woman's menstrual cycle is not extremely regular, or after childbirth when there is no way of knowing when ovulation will begin again. There are too many reasons why a menstrual period may be delayed (including anxiety, sickness, fatigue, etc.) for the calendar alone to be a reliable guide. Using a basal body temperature thermometer in combination with the calendar will increase a woman's chances of knowing when she is ovulating, especially if her periods are very regular anyway.[41] Any couple who seriously wants to consider using the rhythm method to avoid pregnancy should study carefully the details of the method, as described in a book that covers contraception thoroughly. (See "Recommended Reading" at the end of this chapter.)

Male and Female Sterilization

Sterilization is actually the most effective means of contraception. Since the decision to be sterilized is not reversible in most cases, it should be a joint decision. If you are unsure of whether you want to have more children, or if you can't decide which one of you should have the operation, it would be better to wait until you both have a chance to clarify your feelings. Regrets are apt to affect your relationship adversely and can influence the way one or both of you feel about your sexuality. Mixed emotions can certainly be resolved later, but resolving them before you make a decision may save you a lot of trauma and anxiety.

Sterilization procedures involve severing the tubes in men or women to prevent sperm or eggs from moving into the reproductive system and causing pregnancy. In the case of a vasectomy, a small incision is made in the man's scrotum so that the doctor can sever the tubes that carry sperm from the testicles, where they are produced, into the body, where they are combined with other secretions to make up semen. After the operation semen is ejaculated from the penis as usual; only the sperm cells have been eliminated from this fluid. The operation is a simple one, requires only a local anesthetic, and takes less than a half hour.[42] A vasectomy in no way affects the man's sexual characteristics. Other than the slight possibility of side effects secondary to surgery, any changes in his feelings about his sexuality will have a psychological rather than a physical origin.

In the case of tubal ligation, the woman's Fallopian tubes are severed and tied in order to prevent the passage of eggs to the uterus. The least complicated method of performing this operation (called laparoscopic sterilization) involves making a short incision in the abdomen, through which the doctor is able to close off both tubes with special instruments. It requires only a short hospital stay and is sometimes even done on an outpatient basis. Severing a woman's Fallopian tubes has no effect on her secretion of hormones. She continues to menstruate as before; the eggs that are released into the Fallopian tubes gradually disintegrate and are harmlessly absorbed (as are the sperm in the case of a man).[43] Other than the slight possibility of side effects secondary to surgery, any changes she notices in her feelings of sexuality are likewise psychologically rather than physically based.

Advantages of sterilization. Sterilization is almost always effective. Without fear of pregnancy, some couples report an increased enjoyment of sex. Although in some instances it is possible for the doctor to reconnect the tubes that were severed so that the man or woman can become fertile again, there is no guarantee that this can be done. *Thus, it is extremely important that both partners agree that they do not want another pregnancy before either one of them becomes sterilized.*[44]

Disadvantages. For the first six months after a vasectomy, the couple should use another form of contraception. At that time, the man's semen should be examined and declared free of sperm; further contraceptive devices are then unnecessary. Although a vasectomy leaves a man's genital system basically unchanged, some men worry that it will affect their sexual drive, and their anxiety can actually impair their ability to have or keep an erection.[45] It is important that a man be convinced that he wants to have the operation, and that he keep his sense of perspective if he has temporary fears afterwards. It is very helpful to talk to other men who have had a vasectomy and feel good about it.

A woman also may feel uneasy about how sterilization will affect her sexuality or her feelings of adequacy as a woman. She may fear she will be less of a person or less of a sexual partner if she can't become pregnant. Since these feelings can affect her involvement in sex, she, too, should be certain of her decision and will probably find it helpful to talk to other women who have had tubal ligations.

The initial cost of either sterilization procedure is quite high. A vasectomy can cost as much as $100.00 and a tubal ligation is likely to be much more, but some health insurance plans will cover part or all of the cost. Once done, there is no further expense for contraception. Since a tubal ligation (or laparoscopic sterilization) involves surgery, there are some possible complications and postoperative discomfort.[46] It makes sense to ask a doctor more about the procedure he intends to use and to find out the possible aftereffects of the operation itself before actually having it done.

RECOMMENDED READING

Sexuality

The following books might be helpful reading for couples interested in understanding more about sexuality and for anyone having related problems. The Belliveau and Brecher books are more readable, less clinical presentations of Masters and Johnson's studies.

Belliveau, Fred, and Richter, Lin. *Understanding Human Sexual Inadequacy.* New York: Bantam Books, published in arrangement with Little, Brown and Co., 1970.

Brecher, Ruth, and Brecher, Howard, eds. *An Analysis of Human Sexual Response.* New York: New American Library, Signet, 1966.

Masters, William H., and Johnson, Virginia E. *Human Sexual Inadequacy.* Boston: Little, Brown and Co., 1970.

Masters, William H., and Johnson, Virginia E. *Human Sexual Response.* Boston: Little, Brown and Co., 1966.

Birth Control

Boston Women's Health Book Collective. *Our Bodies, Ourselves.* New York: Simon and Schuster, 1971, 1973.

See "Recommending Reading," chapter 1.

Cherniak, Donna, and Feingold, Allan. *Birth Control Handbook.* 11th ed. Montreal: Montreal Health Press, 1973.

This forty-seven-page booklet is an extremely thorough presentation of birth control information. All methods are described in great detail. The booklet is available free from *Birth Control Handbook*, P.O. Box 1000, Station G., Montreal, Quebec, H2W 2N1, Canada. Send $.25 for the first copy and $.10 for each additional copy (maximum ten) to cover shipping costs.

6

Feeling Comfortable
as Parents

BOTH PARENTS ARE UNDER STRESS

Both women and men have feelings about their new situation as parents that may put them mildly or acutely off balance. Becoming comfortable as a mother or father sometimes takes only a few weeks, but often it takes considerably longer. Focusing on the birth as though it were an end in itself and being caught up in making the necessary arrangements may leave you unprepared for the events that follow. Particularly if the birth was a difficult or painful experience, you may feel exhausted and worried about what is ahead. All of a sudden life seems so different. The two of you have to let go of your former relationship and find a way to incorporate a new person into the family. You may feel a sense of loss of the past at the same time that you are hoping the baby will bring new possibilities for the future.

But before the new possibilities can emerge, you may have to sort out and express a lot of feelings that you hadn't anticipated—feelings of anger, resentment, sadness, or disappointment. These are as real and legitimate as the relief, excitement, or happiness that you may also be experiencing. The tendency to idealize babies and parenthood in our culture and the lack of helpful services for new parents leave mothers and fathers feeling very vulnerable when dealing with realities. All too often a new family has to make the adjustment of the first few weeks or months alone, feeling there is nowhere to turn for help. It can come as a shock that caring for a newborn takes so much time and energy; many new parents begin to wonder whether the chaos of the early weeks will become a permanent and impossible way of life for them. Both of you may have a strong urge to escape from the pressures of this difficult time.

Under these circumstances it is hardly surprising if the temptation becomes great to slip into one of the stereotyped roles offered fathers and mothers or to start being unduly influenced by what others seem to expect of you. How can you develop instead a sense of yourselves as parents that grows out of your own feelings? How can you make your family life a flexible experience you both accept and share, rather than an idea in your heads that may not fit your real circumstances? As you begin to readjust your lives, each of you will be influenced by factors from your past and by how you deal with present stress. For women there will be hormonal factors at work. Becoming more aware of your feelings and needs will help both of you find ways to deal with them that are fruitful. Talking with other parents as well as with each other will give you valuable perspective; you may want to explore the possibility of joining a new parents' group.

Although the following discussion of the impact of new parenthood on women and men is presented in separate sections, you will both be intimately involved in the adjustment of the other and deeply affected by it. That is why you need to take interest in each other's feelings and support each other.

DYNAMICS OF NEW MOTHERS' FEELINGS

The Initial Impact of Motherhood

Your reaction to motherhood may be different than you had imagined. The range of feelings women have after childbirth is great because there are so many factors involved: your general physical condition, how prepared you were for the birth, what your pain threshold is and what kind of medication you had (if any), what sort of labor and delivery you had, how much support you had from your husband or others, your own personality, and the state of your hormones. At some point you may want to think more about your own experience. If it went well, why? What can you learn from it that might be helpful for another birth? If it didn't go well, are there factors you could change another time? Later on you may well forget the details and remember only your strong feelings, whether positive or negative.

In addition to the enormous psychological impact of suddenly becoming a mother, your body is simultaneously undergoing a marked hormonal readjustment. You had probably heard about "baby blues" before your child was born, and you may even have paused a moment to consider how the blues might affect you. Many women, though, find that they are very unprepared for the ups and downs that actually occur. Determined as you may be to make the adjustment to motherhood with few tears and no hysteria, it isn't always that easy. The hormones that were necessary to sustain your pregnancy are undergoing rapid change now that your baby and the placenta have been delivered. It often takes several weeks before you regain the hormonal balance and emotional stability you are accustomed to having.

While still in the hospital, some women experience severe doubt about their whole situation and fear that they cannot or don't want to care for their babies. If you expected to feel elated, you may be all the more upset to find yourself anxious, discouraged, or depressed. If you do have negative feelings in the hospital, it may be difficult to find the reassurance and help you need, and it is understandable that you may feel guilty or afraid.

Rather than having specific fears or doubts, other women may simply feel moody and irritable. There is a tendency to become upset very easily during this time and to cry periodically without obvious cause. While these feelings may begin in the hospital, they may well continue on and off for several weeks or more after returning home.

Even if your body weren't undergoing marked hormonal adjustments, your life has indisputably changed overnight. At a time when you probably feel emotionally and physically exhausted, you are suddenly confronted with feelings for which you may be unprepared—about yourself as a mother, about your baby, and about your husband. You may feel unsure of how quickly you will recuperate, and you may feel unusually dependent on others, possibly even intimidated by them. Ironically, at the time when you most need to be cared for, you become painfully aware of how totally dependent your tiny baby is on you. On the one hand you may experience a sense of peace, tranquility, and satisfaction; on the other hand you may be overwhelmed by a disquieting degree of ambivalence and turmoil. Your whole life may seem bound up with the baby, and you may suddenly feel confused and confined.

The strength of your initial feelings makes it hard to see your situation objectively. At times you may feel others are judging your worth as an individual by how happy you seem to be as a mother. Part of you wants to appear strong, take things in your stride, and be applauded for your marvelous adjustment to motherhood. But then you must try to hide the other feelings you may have—the letdown, resentment, or even anger that can result from the changes in your life and the demands being made on you. Under these pressures it is often impossible to know what is really wrong or why you are upset. The apparent reasons are usually as minor as the phone waking the baby or interrupting your bath or your husband returning five minutes later than you had expected. Suddenly they loom large and seem to threaten totally the semblance of order and control you thought you had achieved and so desperately want.

Actually the strong feelings you are trying so hard to keep under the surface are finally claiming the attention they deserve. As the tears you have been fighting off finally begin to flow, you may feel like a child yourself and wonder who will take care of you and help you. You may feel terribly vulnerable and fear you are falling apart. Letting these feelings out in all of their intensity may seem too threatening to you, but expressing them is the only way to release them. They are real and human, and you need to be held and comforted just as your baby does. Once you have let yourself cry, you'll feel like an adult and a mother again; holding the feelings back was what made them seem so frightening and overpowering. Now you can go on with a new appreciation for the intensity of that part of you and perhaps also with a better understanding of the strong feelings your husband and baby will sometimes show. Admitting and confronting your feelings as they occur will keep them from building up to a point where you feel you can't handle them.

You need plenty of rest. Coping with intense feelings will be much harder if you are exhausted. Having at least one real rest period a day for the first several weeks, or longer, will make a great deal of difference in your ability to handle the daily stress and strain. If you are nursing, make a point of lying down for feedings or at least be sure to make yourself comfortable. If you seem to be getting more and more tired, and the baby isn't taking a long predictable nap each day, arrange to have someone help you while you get a long period of undisturbed sleep. This will probably make an enormous difference in your outlook and will be a good experience for whoever takes over.

Simplify the housework. Another important step you can take is to simplify the housework and re-examine your standards of cleanliness and neatness. Decide which things could be eliminated altogether, at least temporarily. Forget about elaborate meals for now, and rely on frozen foods, take-out dinners, and paper plates whenever possible. If you ever plan to get such appliances as a washing machine, clothes dryer, or dishwasher, now is when you need them most. If you can't afford them, perhaps friends will take a load of clothes to the Laundromat or home to their own machines when you don't feel up to doing the wash yourself. Diaper service, if you can afford it for even a few weeks or months, can be a real energy saver. Ask about economy rates using older but just as sterile diapers. Or, if you are planning to do your own diapers but can afford the disposable kind for a couple of weeks, you will probably find it well worth the extra expense. Some parents feel that diaper liners save a lot of work.

Learn to be ingenious about fitting light housework into the time your baby is awake when you can talk or sing to her as you work. Put her near you while you wash the dishes, for example, or carry her in a sling or a pack while you do a quick job of vacuuming or dusting. Some new parents find it helps to view housework as a series of very small tasks, rather than several large ones. Instead of feeling frustrated because you never have enough time to clean a whole room, aim instead to do only one part of the job. If, for example, you are annoyed by the mess in the kitchen, put the dishes into some water to soak, and then relax for a while while you read the paper or feed the baby. If you plan to do only a portion of the entire job, you won't be so frustrated by the inevitable interruptions. As many new parents have learned the hard way, this is not the time for compulsive housecleaning.

Coming to Terms with Changes

Your initial strong reactions to motherhood are only part of what is happening in your life. You are also having to adjust to the inevitable changes that having a baby brings. In the back of your mind you may hope that they are only temporary, and that within a few weeks or months you'll easily be able to have a life of your own, share a full relationship with your husband, and be a mother as well. If you have always been able to accomplish most of what you wanted to do, you probably assumed that this feeling of being able to control your time would return shortly. It can be a real blow if after three, four, or even six weeks have passed, you discover that your life just isn't working out that way. At this point you may be tempted to hide your real feelings in a desperate attempt to seem satisfied with the way motherhood is turning out for you.

No matter how enthralled you were about becoming a mother, it doesn't take long to discover that you were poorly prepared to cope with the day-to-day disappointments and frustrations that are bound to occur, especially if you are often home alone with your baby. Particularly at first, a great deal of time is spent caring for her—feeding, bathing, changing diapers, washing clothes, holding, and soothing. You may be going out of your way to keep the baby's things from taking over the house and to create the relaxing atmosphere of your pre-baby days. All this can be unbelievably time-consuming, and you may find it hard to explain where your days are going.

The daily routine of a new mother can indeed present a real challenge to her sense of self. When a woman begins to feel that her day adds up to nothing for herself, when she is living from dishes to bed-making to feeding the baby to shopping to preparing dinner to collapsing, with more of the same to look forward to the next day, she may well feel dissatisfied no matter how important her family is to her.

Feeling Disoriented

At about this time various experiences you may have in the course of an ordinary day may begin to make you wonder further about yourself. They are relatively funny when you realize how many new mothers share them, but they can be upsetting if you aren't aware of how common they are. You may hear nonexistent cries, for instance. As you step into the shower, you may realize that if your baby needed you, you wouldn't even know it. You are suddenly so sure you hear her cry that you turn off the water to check. You were mistaken. You turn the water on again, hurrying a little now. Again you hear crying and turn off the water. Again there is silence. The same thing can happen while you are washing the dishes, or in those daring moments when you step outside to get the milk or mail.

Maybe you find yourself constantly peeking into your baby's room during naptime or at night to be sure she is still breathing. Though desperate for an unbroken night's sleep, you may find that as the baby begins to sleep for longer periods, you continue to wake up and may even get up to check on her. Eventually, as your confidence grows and you become more experienced, you will lose these feelings of anxiety.

You may find that you easily forget things—simple things, like what you were just looking for, doing, or thinking about. You may even forget that your baby is asleep in the next room and almost set out for the store or to visit a friend. Maybe you lock yourself out of the house when you have never done so before. When you talk to friends, your words may come out garbled. You feel as though you cannot carry on a coherent conversation, or express yourself well. You actually begin to wonder whether you are still capable of thinking!

Perhaps this whole phenomenon is related to how easily distracted you are, with so many different things on your mind and so many demands being made on you. If you are tired and disoriented, it isn't surprising that your thought processes and thinking abilities are temporarily shaky. It is frustrating to discover that every time you begin to think about something, you are distracted. And once interrupted, you may find you are unable to return to that thought or state of mind.

Mixed Feelings and Expectations

As you begin to discover how little time you have to yourself and how unsure you sometimes feel of your ability to function as an adult, you are probably also experiencing some strong feelings about your husband that you may be reluctant to express. Although you are both parents of this child, he may seem much less affected by the baby than you are, much less tied down and preoccupied with her. He may not seem to recognize the extent to which your life has changed or be as interested in the details of your day with the baby as you would like. (If your whole day is spent on details, the least he could do is seem fascinated!) Actually he may be partly reacting against what he sees as a total and unnecessary preoccupation with the baby on your part. Being constantly worried and involved with the baby—never wanting to go out alone or let the baby cry, or think of yourselves first—can be a way of avoiding dealing with your husband's feelings. Or perhaps he is very sympathetic and says he is willing to help you, but you are getting the impression that actually he resents pitching in. Or maybe you just can't bring yourself to suggest that you really need some help when he arrives home looking tired or depressed. You may hesitate to ask him to take over the baby or make dinner, though you may want to. If you do the work yourself, you may later resent him. But if you ask for help, you may feel that he resents you. These feelings may seem too strong and too explosive to deal with, so you fluctuate between nobly trying to do everything yourself, and retreating from all the work by being openly angry or by giving some excuse that seems more acceptable. Either way, you may feel guilty or embarrassed about the way you are acting and feeling.

One way to avoid the confusion and get away from these uncomfortable feelings is to choose one of the stereotyped roles offered women in this country in magazines, on television, and by other mothers who are having similar problems dealing with their feelings. The "motherhood-is-all-fulfilling" approach encourages you to convince yourself that all of your needs can be met by mothering. You may decide on the "homemade misery" role; as long as you're home anyway, you might as well be a natural mother who totally breast-feeds her baby, bakes all the family's bread, sews, knits, and gets all her chores done before her husband gets home. The "full-time martyr," on the other hand, realizes that life with a baby is difficult but feels it is her duty to assume full responsibility and sees no way to change her situation. To make her daily sacrifices more bearable, she talks lightly of her struggles and good deeds and decides on being serenely unhappy. Meanwhile "super-mom" jumps back into her profession a few weeks after childbirth, feeling no conflicts. She is a stunning spare-time mother and gourmet cook, and just can't understand how other mothers get themselves into such ruts. There are other alternatives open to you as well, such as following in the footsteps of your own mother or a close friend.

There is nothing wrong with being a full-time mother, making homemade bread, totally breast-feeding your baby, being natural, devoted, or combining a profession with motherhood. But if you adopt a ready-made role because you are afraid to deal with your own feelings and conflicts and are reluctant to find out what your husband's feelings really are, sooner or later you are likely to resent both yourself and your husband —and your child as well. Recognizing all your feelings (positive and negative) and finding ways to express them without concluding that you are a failure or that you were not cut out to be a mother can free you to discover what kind of mother you really want to be, and can open up the infinite possibilities for personal growth that parenthood can bring.

In *The Growth and Development of Mothers,* Angela Barron McBride points out, "You will never be able to stop having negative feelings, but you can start appreciating their diagnostic value; they are trying to tell you something about yourself."[1] If you are feeling inadequate or resentful, try to find out why. Do you need more time to yourself? Is there more work than you can handle alone? Until you and your husband can get out in the open your feelings and expectations of each other and of yourselves without being afraid of what will happen to your family, neither of you will be able to go ahead and experiment with the style of parenthood that really suits you. The alternative is too often to adopt one of the ready-made roles and spend your time playing it out. Then you are apt to become concerned with pleasing others and set your standards according to their notion of the right way. You may find yourself constantly comparing yourself to other mothers, who may be doing exactly what you are, and comparing your baby to other babies, preoccupied underneath with whether or not you are measuring up. You never feel free to express the full range of your feelings because you are afraid that sensing a conflict between your own needs as a person and the demands of motherhood means you are a bad mother. Trying to hide these feelings makes you resentful and angry and leads to frustration. Hiding your bad feelings may also make you less free to be close to your husband and relax with him; you are afraid of what will happen when you are off your guard and let your feelings flow freely. But if you accept the whole range of your feelings and find out how to meet the needs they reflect, you will no longer need to rely on stereotypes and you will begin to learn what it takes to be the kind of mother you want to be.

Your Need for Adult Companionship

Part of the problem of letdown that some new mothers feel grows out of their increased isolation. You are not as mobile now as you once were. If you don't soon plan to return to a job or other activity, you may have to make a special effort to maintain contact with other adults. For the first few weeks, while regaining your strength, you need to limit your visits with friends and relatives. After that it becomes a matter of logistics: inviting friends over or figuring out ways of transporting yourself and your baby to places where you can be with other adults you find interesting and stimulating. Some women feel the need to get out and be with friends more acutely than others. But all women need at least some outside contacts. Seeing other people and sharing your concerns with them gives you an important perspective on yourself and your capabilities. It is perhaps more important now than ever to keep that perspective. You are a person with thoughts and ideas about a great variety of subjects. And it is likely that you need contact with other adults—away from home and its problems—in order to continue to grow as a person.

Even if you are new in the community, there are ways you can solve the problem of isolation. While it may take real effort and determination on your part, doing so may keep you from feeling trapped. In nice weather make a point of taking walks around your neighborhood and stopping to talk with the people who live nearby. If you can get to a park or other gathering place, you will surely find other parents of young children. Ask about places of interest in the area or find out whether there are groups for young parents in the community. Also check the local paper for listings of groups for new parents or new mothers (postpartum groups), or other activities that sound interesting. If you have a hobby or interest, find out where you could pursue it locally. Whatever else happens, keep trying until you find some source of meaningful contact with other adults.

On the other hand, if you already have friends in the area, begin resuming contact with them as soon as you feel the need. Don't sit around waiting for someone to call you. All too often, what seems to happen is that people who feel isolated (for whatever reason) tend to withdraw and wait for someone else to sense their need for help. Don't let yourself fall into that pattern. Take the initiative of asking a friend to visit you or of telling a friend that you are feeling low and need to get out. Especially if your baby's fussiness is really upsetting you, you'll feel better if you have someone to talk to. In nice weather, go out as often as you can, for a walk around the block or a trip to the store. Simply getting out of the house and seeing other adults, even if you don't know them personally, will boost your morale and give you some perspective.

With or without your own means of transportation you can stay in touch with other adults. If you have a car or have a friend with a car, think about possible trips to museums, parks, zoos, or shopping centers. Or decide to become an expert on the resources of your own city or town, including the available public transportation. Keep in mind all the useful baby-carrying devices that are now available. Disposable diapers, bottles of prepared formula, and jars of baby food can be used anywhere and will make your brief or extended outings much easier.

Readiness for Outside Involvement

Many women who don't want or need to work are hesitant about undertaking outside involvements. There are many reasons for this: lack of confidence, uncertainty about leaving the baby, problems finding a baby-sitter, or just not knowing what kind of involvement would be most satisfying.

You may have to do a good deal of experimenting to find out what you really want. It probably won't help to rush from your home in a desperate attempt to get away from it all. Try to consider the alternatives during one of your less hassled moments. While your family and friends can be helpful sources of ideas and important sounding boards for your thoughts and concerns, don't let anyone pressure you into making more of a commitment than you feel ready for. Even if you kick yourself later for letting uncertainties stand in your way, try to respect your own sense of readiness for outside involvements. Perhaps you could begin in a small way, such as by taking an interesting class for a couple of hours a week for a month or two. See how the baby-sitting arrangements work out, how you feel about leaving the baby, and what effect your getting out on a regular basis has on you. Be confident that as the need arises, you will be able to find meaningful activities; there is no need to feel desperate or pressured. The more aware you become of your needs, the more certainty you will have that you can find a way to meet them.

Once you are committed to finding your own way as a mother, you are likely to feel more comfortable. You'll become aware of your feelings and needs a few at a time, and you'll have many practical problems to work out as you seek to fulfill those needs. Once you have found a way to arrange for some time to yourself (see chapter 2, "Finding Baby-sitters"), you'll be freer to explore the possibilities in your new life. If you plan to go back to work right away, talk with other new parents who have been in a similar situation, and ask for their recommendations for finding day care or other baby-sitting arrangements. They may be able to help with other problems that develop as well. Even if the process takes longer than you expected, stick with your plans and don't lose confidence in yourself. If your focus is clear and you are recognizing your feelings, you'll be able to overcome any obstacles you face more easily.

Serious Postpartum Depression

Feeling low, discouraged, or depressed from time to time is normal, as is wondering whether you'll make it through a difficult afternoon or an impossible evening. All new mothers have their bad days and feel as if they may not be able to cope any longer. Fortunately, in most cases a good rest or a change of scene will alleviate those feelings, and you are then more optimistic about the future.

You may begin to have extreme feelings, however, that indicate a need for outside help. The extremes may be low or high. You may feel very sad, hopeless, and negative, or you may be terribly high, constantly getting new insights into yourself and others and feeling you must talk excessively, to the point where you can't stop and relax. In either case your mood will begin to interfere with eating, sleeping, and caring for your baby. You may find yourself becoming restless, irritable, incoherent, or concerned with trivialities. If rest and sleep don't reverse these symptoms of emotional strain, or you are unable to fall asleep so your fatigue grows even worse, you are apt to panic. You may feel so overwhelmed that you fear you will do something to hurt either yourself or your baby.

Serious postpartum disturbances are not common, but they do occur. Recent theories about their cause emphasize the physical and social stress that new mothers experience. Physical stress theories are based on studies that seem to link postpartum depression with thyroid difficulties and/or with the hormonal imbalance that occurs at the end of pregnancy when the levels of estrogen and progesterone are dramatically reduced. Drugs such as thyroid compounds, tranquilizers and anti-depressants, and hormonal treatment are sometimes prescribed.[2] Social stress theories emphasize the degree of conflict a mother feels about her new role, the amount of emotional support and practical help she has, and the extent of her isolation. Traumatic past experiences like the death of the wife's mother or husband's father, fear, failure, incomplete education, a history of pregnancy complications in the wife's family, or lack of experience with babies may also be significant. The more of these stresses a woman is under, according to one study, the more difficult her postpartum adjustment will be.[3]

If you feel you are not making a satisfactory adjustment, and you have begun recognizing the extreme feelings mentioned above, see your doctor and talk over the situation with him. If he can't help, ask for the name of someone who can, or investigate other possibilities yourself. Crisis clinics, mental health clinics, and family counselors or therapists will be able to help you decide on appropriate support and possibly treatment. Don't give up until you find someone who will listen sympathetically and take your problem seriously.

FATHERS HAVE CONFLICTS TOO

Fathers All React Differently

Whatever your thoughts were as you anticipated becoming a father, your actual feelings following the birth may come as a surprise. A man who has taken childbirth preparation classes and has participated in the birth of his baby may feel higher and more excited than ever in his life. Whether the birth was difficult and traumatic or easier than expected, he has been able to support his wife and has shared in the awe and relief of going through the experience firsthand. Talking to relatives and friends adds to his general excitement and provides a chance to relive the experience, and waking up at home for the first time with the baby there may bring a renewed sense of amazement: "Wow—this is *real*, the baby is *ours!*"

Another man may have a totally different reaction and may even be embarrassed by all the fuss; to him it seems overdone. Calling gushy relatives makes him feel uncomfortable, and he may be uneasy about the kind of excitement everyone seems to expect from him. His honest reaction to the birth is happy but matter-of-fact, low-key, and quiet. If his wife and baby seem healthy and are resting, that is all he expected or hoped for. It may not occur to him to press his wife for feelings she does not volunteer on her own. He notices the baby but feels uncomfortable fussing over her; he is not sure whether there is any need for him to relate to a baby so young and still so unable to respond. If overpowering relatives enter at this point and "ooh" and "ahh" over the baby and then take over sympathetically but firmly as though they know what this is all about, this father may feel like an outsider and wonder, "Is all this commotion really necessary? Of course it is exciting; now let's get on with the business of raising a family."

There is a wide range of reactions to fatherhood and it's hard to say what your initial feelings mean. They are partly related to your degree of involvement in the birth, partly a matter of personal style, and they may also reflect deeper feelings you are just beginning to be aware of now that you are a father. You may have a harder time sorting through your feelings if relatives are around the house a great deal. Although you are probably grateful for the extra help with the baby and household work, you may feel useless and unable to try anything your own way for as long as they are there. There may never seem to be a chance for you to be by yourself or alone with your wife, or to get a sense of what your baby is like.

Dealing with Practical Realities

No matter how you feel in the first few weeks after the birth, the time from about the third to the sixth week is apt to be particularly difficult. You are probably alone as a family again, relatives aren't around, and friends are visiting less. This is when the practical realities begin to hit you.

These realities vary with each new father. Possibly you feel pressured to take your work more seriously, maybe you are suddenly hit with the expenses that have been piling up, or you feel you've got to finish up projects you have neglected for a long time. There is a lot of baby care and extra housework to be done. Going somewhere may become a major production, and you may always be the one who has to carry the car bed, diaper bag, extra food and clothes, etc.

You may feel immobilized by the activities at home and find it hard to get away, back to outside work. Or you may feel eager to return to the outside world which assures you a wider focus. You may begin to get angry when the baby wakes up a lot and you can't get enough sleep, or annoyed that the times when you are home—no matter what your work schedule—are so confused, noisy, and exhausting. If your wife seems tired and depressed when you come home, you may begin to wonder impatiently how long it is going to take her to adjust; it is harder to be sympathetic to her feelings when the atmosphere at home is starting to get you down. You may begin to nod absently or withdraw when she is eager to explain how things are going with the baby. You may feel that you have no time to yourself, no chance for quiet or solitude or to do the things that are important to you. If you have convinced yourself at some point that this baby is not going to change your life, these day-to-day realities may hit you hard and make you have real doubts about the way things are working out.

These are feelings that many fathers share, and their intensity is closely related to the temperaments of all the family members, especially the baby. Some babies simply give their parents more peace and rest than others (see "Babies Have Different Temperaments" in chapter 2). How you feel depends partly on how tired you are and how much confusion and noise you are able to tolerate. It's one thing if the changes are hitting you gradually and you are fairly rested; it's another if you are suddenly dealing with a baby who cries eight to ten hours a day, or who is active and demanding and rarely sleeps.

Until you get to know your baby better, it is hard to start rearranging your lives so there is more space and time for everyone. But this is only part of the problem. Babies bring out aspects of their parents that are new: when you bring an infant home there is not just one new person to get to know, there are three. Facing up to the fact that all of your lives are changing may help you let go of life as it used to be and become more involved in how things are developing in the present. The kind of father you become can grow out of an awareness of yourself in your new situation. Thinking more about your feelings toward your wife as she is now and about your baby as you get to know her better will help you see your own feelings more clearly. And the more you and your wife understand about each other's feelings and share them, the more you'll be able to help each other in dealing with the present rather than escaping into fantasies of better days, ignoring the real problems, or getting in each other's way.

Feelings about Your Wife

You need to understand all you can about how your wife feels about herself, the baby, and you. But it's just as important to bring your feelings about her into focus, because you'll learn a lot about yourself in the process. No matter how understanding you want to be about the amount of time your wife is spending with the baby compared with the time and energy she has left for you, by the time three or four weeks have gone by, you are probably beginning to resent it a little or a lot. This may be even more true if your wife is breast-feeding. Even if you strongly support the decision to breast-feed, there may be times when you feel it makes too many demands on her and seems to give the baby priority over you in every aspect of your relationship. When you feel like this, resentment about breast-feeding may get lumped together with other feelings: annoyance at the changes the baby has made in your life, anger about your lack of peace and quiet, or frustration over the lack of time you have with your wife for relaxation or sexual enjoyment. You may feel sad or angry about the loss of your old relationship with her and even wonder whether she cares enough or has time (or if you do) to start a new relationship. If you feel tension about wanting to be together, yet being pulled apart, you may be tempted to blame her and/or the baby. When you are together you may feel unsure how to begin to get involved with each other. Your wife may be anxious to tell you how she feels, but you may find it hard to listen if you are frustrated or resentful underneath. And the more you sense her anxiety, the more hesitant you may be to express your own.

Much as you may really want to talk with her and get things straightened out, the temptation may also be great to choose one of the many escape routes open to men. You may take off with your friends and talk about "women's work" and how "the honeymoon is over—it's all downhill from here," or begin to see your wife as a little girl playing mama with her doll and decide not to take her problems seriously. You may begin to slip into the "breadwinner" mentality: your wife and baby should make no demands on you, the head of the family, at least until the child needs a father to deal with important decisions—discipline, guidance, knowledge of the real world. Maybe you seriously wonder whether something is wrong with your wife. Why isn't she idyllically happy and taking care of everything the way she is supposed to be? Isn't she the one who wanted this baby to begin with? After all, you are holding up your end of the bargain. Why is she so inadequate that you need to do so much?

From a distance these reactions may seem funny or insulting, but when the confusion continues and you aren't sure what to do about it, avoiding the realities at home may be more tempting than you expect. The trouble is that these are not solutions at all. They take you away from the present, away from your own feelings, and away from your wife and baby. Avoiding issues because they are complex and uncomfortable, or because it seems easier and safer to ignore them, will make matters worse at home. If you are dealing with your own feelings and your wife's and are coming to terms with your baby, you are taking the most straightforward approach you can to move ahead. Your willingness to get involved will greatly affect how soon you grow close again.

So take the risk, express your feelings to your wife if you can. Say what's bothering you and listen to what is bothering her, so you can go on together and work things out. And try not to get bogged down and forget how much you want to understand and accept each other and be closer. The effort may be hard to make at first, but if it gets you where you want to be with each other, you'll be glad you made it.

Remember that the amount of household work has increased a lot and you are both tired. Whenever possible, help each other relax; but do it together, or make sure you each have enough turns. When you are both tired and not in the mood to deal with the baby or each other, try to confront the conflict openly, negotiate, and find a compromise that you can both accept. Take turns talking and listening so one of you doesn't go on and on and end up talking to yourself—you need each other. Try to be practical about saving time on routine tasks like dinner and dishes. Keep small things small, and save most of your energy for growing together and finding time for each of you to be alone. If you can keep your priorities straight, you'll all feel life smoothing out, and you'll begin seeing the humor and possibilities in your new family sooner.

Mama's Little Baby

A crucial problem that needs to be resolved if you are to be close as a couple and if you are going to be free to get to know your baby is the sensitive question of whose baby this is, anyway. Theoretically it's not a problem at all. But many men get blatant or subtle messages from their wives which say either "hands off—this is my turf," or "please help—I'll show you the right way to relate to the baby, what to do when she cries, how to give her a bath, how to put on her pj's,"—possibly down to the minutest detail of matching the diaper pins so they are color-coordinated. Your wife may not want to do this, or she may be unaware that she is doing it: you can help by getting the problem out in the open where it can be dealt with.

Opening up is not easy, especially if your wife is already tense and exhausted and you realize that bringing up the subject may make matters worse. But the alternatives may make the risk worthwhile; either you get involved her way or you gradually leave her to her turf and retreat to ground that is less frustrating. The price of either choice is high. If you turn more and more of your energy to outside involvements and start spending less time at home, you are jeopardizing your closeness with both your wife and your baby. (Her version of this is to become so preoccupied with the baby that she is never willing to get out and forget about being a mother.) If you decide to go along with your wife's approach, you may feel uncomfortable and judged; it will be hard to develop a relationship you like with your baby, and you're bound to resent your wife for putting you in such a position. Either way you remain an outsider instead of a full participant in the family.

The irony is that very possibly your wife is feeling put off by the number of people telling her how to relate to the baby. Then why does she feel she must tell you? If your initial reactions to the baby seem quite different from hers, she may feel that allowing you to be "right" makes her "wrong" in some way. She is probably partly expressing feelings she has had since childhood that she ought to know what to do with a baby and how to do it. Part of her may feel like a little girl trying to play mama with her doll. If she has taken care of many children in the past and been told she is good at it, these feelings may be particularly strong. No matter what her reasons are for giving you messages that this is her baby (and she may not be aware of her reasons), try to remember that it may not be a question of a well-thought-out conviction that she holds. Many feelings from her past have been triggered by the present situation, and they are probably stronger because she is tired and trying her best to cope with the new and confusing job of being a mother. She wants to do well, she wants to give you and others confidence in her. Motherhood is new to her and probably not at all what she thought it would be like. Her doubts about herself and the pressure she is under may make her lose perspective about your involvement with the baby. In fact, you may lose perspective too at times and begin expecting your wife to be the kind of mother that you imagine would make your life easier.

Whether you confront the matter verbally or simply decide to ignore her messages and proceed on the assumption that there are many ways of relating to your baby, one way or another you really need to help get across the message that each of you needs to handle the baby in your own way. Hovering over each other and rushing in to save the day when the baby cries and the other parent is taking care of her makes you self-conscious and preoccupied with how well you are doing your job. Having confidence in each other's style from the beginning makes an enormous difference in how involved you both become and how much friction there is between you about the baby. It also makes your family more flexible.

Your Own Style of Fatherhood

If you have thought a little about your initial reaction to becoming a father, explored your feelings toward your wife, and then moved on to establish that you are both parents with your own approach to life and to babies, you are already on your way to becoming a father in your own style. But there are still many demands on your time and energy, and you may find that ambivalence about being a father recurs periodically. How often your doubts surface will depend on how hard the job is for you, considering your total circumstances—the demands of your work, other activities, your relationship with your wife, pulls on her time, the temperament of your baby, and so on.

As you first get to know your baby, you may at times feel your wife has an unfair advantage; she was developing a relationship in utero and had the first few days to get to know the baby before you could discover what being alone with a newborn is like. If she is breast-feeding, she also has the special satisfaction of knowing she is meeting one of the baby's most basic needs. Some men feel helpless and frustrated by not being able to be involved in feeding. If you feel that way, perhaps the two of you can decide that you will give the baby an occasional bottle of breast milk or formula.

There are plenty of other needs you can explore with your baby. If you have started spending time with her, you will have begun to improvise and will be discovering for yourself what she is like. When your wife is around, it may seem harder to communicate with the baby. She often seems pulled to her mother as though to a magnet, and you have to pull her away again before you can establish any rapport. At times like this it is best to take the baby to a different room or outside for a while until you get started relating to each other. Many fathers find that they enjoy being with their children more when they are on their own. It may be more fun to hold and feed your baby, give her a bath, or take her for a walk by yourself without feeling you are being observed or possibly judged by others. Some fathers are tense about fussing and crying; others aren't. In either case you are apt to relax more after you have dealt with it in your own way a few times and learned from experience what you want to do about different kinds of crying. You can also develop your own way of talking to your baby. When you start getting a response and feel that the two of you are communicating, you'll begin to feel that the effort to get to know her is worth it. The promise of pleasure is as great for you as it is for your wife if you discover that you can forget yourself and be unself-consciously sensitive and responsive to your child.

But like any relationship, it won't be all rosy. Fathers who are involved sometimes have to cope with babies who are fussy and impossible, and there will be days when you are impatient and too tired to make the effort to get through to your baby. Try as you may to compromise and be generous about rearranging your schedule for the baby's sake, some babies aren't very gracious about letting you get a reasonable amount of rest and quiet. At times you'll resent your baby, and she'll make you really angry. You may start to feel she never even gives you the chance to sit down and relax or talk to your wife. These are the times when you'll begin to feel real pulls on your time and be aware of how many things you would like to do but no longer have time for.

At this point you may be tempted to retreat to the views of fatherhood you grew up with. You may be sensitive, for example, to the fact that most baby care books are addressed to mothers, and that many people still assume that men aren't suited to care for young babies and shouldn't be involved with children until later on. Perhaps you remember your father bragging about the fact that he never took care of you or changed your diaper, and you realize what a major commitment to your new family you have already made. When you are frustrated by fatherhood, your present involvement may seem like a mistake. Actually your wife (who probably grew up with the idea that she would find total fulfillment in motherhood) probably feels the same way when she is upset. If you are tolerant of each other's feelings, you can help each other devise an approach to your baby that is more fair for everyone and allows both of you to get away from the confusion for some privacy. You'll both be better off if you trust your present family rather than retreat to the ideas you once had of the way a family should work out. Maybe you are also ready to take the important step of finding someone else you can count on to take care of your baby so you can get away together. Being parents is hard work, and needing breaks to get back in touch with friends or activities you haven't had time for (or back in touch with yourself) is not escaping; on the contrary, it is essential for keeping up your morale and energy.

NEEDING HELP IS LEGITIMATE

The two of you may want to think about what kinds of support will keep you going if you aren't able to find solutions to the problems you face. It usually helps a lot if each of you can count on sympathetic friends to relax with and get new perspective. When you both have strong needs, being listened to and appreciated by others may make it easier for you to regain the good humor you need to go ahead together sympathetically as a couple and as parents.

But if parenthood seems discouraging to one or both of you, and you are beginning to avoid the problems at home, you might also want to consider talking to a counselor. Some parents are reluctant to take this step, feeling they should be able to solve their own problems. Others may be unaware that counseling is a very different matter than it used to be. Some health plans include free counseling as part of their services, for example, assuming that it is something many men and women might want to take advantage of at some point or other in their lives. Counseling is more often viewed now as a temporary way to help you get through a crisis than an indication that you have deep or serious problems. Times of stress (such as birth and the postpartum period) have been recognized as times of tremendous potential growth. But being pressured by circumstances to change more quickly than you find comfortable or even tolerable may make you want to withdraw and close up. Getting support from a counselor is a way of giving yourself a chance to catch up with the changes so you won't be overwhelmed. A trained person can reflect back to you your own feelings so you'll see them more clearly and quickly, and you'll be able to decide what you can do to cope with your situation in a way that makes you feel better.

If you have friends you trust and who are sympathetic, you may prefer to discuss the situation with them. But keep in mind that they may find it very hard to be as objective or as patient as someone who has been trained to assume this role. If you can recognize that needing support is legitimate, you'll be able to decide what kind of help is most appropriate in your circumstances. If you are interested in seeing a counselor, you could call a community mental health clinic or ask your family doctor for a recommendation, if that makes you feel more comfortable.

As time goes on your family life will probably smooth out and become much more enjoyable, but problems will continue to come up now and then. Both men and women sometimes panic and want to escape when they feel stifled at home. The need to be fully yourself, at home and away from home, is legitimate for both fathers and mothers. Neither of you will be happy if being parents ties you down completely. The exciting thing is to realize that you can do many of the things you want to if you are open with each other about your needs and are willing to experiment with new ways of arranging your lives.

GROUPS FOR NEW PARENTS

It takes time to feel comfortable as parents and to arrange your lives in a way that you both feel satisfied with. Talking with other new parents helps you get perspective and explore your own feelings more fully, and it also exposes you to a wider range of problems and of possibilities. Groups for new parents offer information and sometimes practical support and can help you develop an approach to problems that takes everyone's needs into account.

New parents' groups are gradually becoming available across the country. The groups have a variety of focuses and formats, but all aim to help parents open up about the problems they face in the postpartum time and to work for solutions to these problems. Most are informal gatherings with an atmosphere of mutual sharing.

If you are interested in finding out whether there are groups in your community, try calling the local childbirth education groups, any organizations that offer help with breast-feeding, parent education groups, or your local hospitals or community mental health centers. Or, try asking a Public Health nurse (or call the Department of Health), your doctor, or the Family Life Department of a community college. You may find that the resources of your community are greater than you first thought. If no groups are already organized, consider talking again to any people in these organizations who have seemed interested in the idea, and ask them to consider making new parents' groups available. You might offer to help recruit parents you know to discuss their needs further with these professionals.

If you can't generate any interest among people in these organizations, consider starting an informal group on your own. Meet with any friends who share your concern and at least sit down together for an evening and think about the possibilities. Are there ways you could help each other, or other new parents, with mutual concerns, like baby-sitting and sharing baby equipment? Are you interested in getting outside resource people to fill you in on aspects of parenthood you'd like to know more about? Do you think you could help each other with some of the more personal problems that are bothering you? If the interest seems to be great enough, try to set up regular meetings, once a month to start with, and see what happens. If the group falls apart, at least you have begun being more open with other families, and you have a small idea of some of the problems other parents face.

If your group continues to meet, you will probably find that as you get to know each other better, you will gradually begin sharing your personal problems and concerns as parents. Such a group can be of great practical help to all of you as you look for solutions to common problems such as starting a baby-sitting co-op, sharing outdoor play equipment for children of various ages, organizing play groups when your babies are older, finding a community building for an indoor tot-lot for winter play, sharing names of baby-sitters, and so on. Before you had a child, you may not have seen the need for friends to share these common practical concerns. But now you may begin to see how everyone can benefit from the community you build around your needs as families. Sharing makes all of your lives more flexible and more fun.

RECOMMENDED READING

Boston Women's Health Book Collective. *Our Bodies, Ourselves.* New York: Simon and Schuster, 1971, 1973.

Contains a sympathetic discussion of the postpartum period, including "Possible Causes of Postpartum Disturbance," pp. 209–17.

Chess, Stella; Thomas, Alexander; and Birch, Herbert G. *Your Child Is a Person.* New York: Viking Press, 1965.

Contains a helpful chapter on the subject of going back to work, entitled "The Working Mother: Not Guilty!" pp. 166–72.

McBride, Angela Barron. *The Growth and Development of Mothers.* New York: Harper and Row, 1973.

Angela Barron McBride emphasizes the interrelation between the growth and development of mothers and of babies and suggests that parenthood is a role you grow into by understanding your own behavior and learning how to handle your needs. She explores the critical issues she feels a mother must be aware of in her own life to help her child develop: the complex expectations of self, family, and society; the struggle with emotions like anger, depression, guilt, and ambivalence; and sexuality, discussed in relation to the Oedipal-Electra period of a child's development. McBride points out that all of these issues are confused by their relation to the thinking of the community-at-large, so that a "grown-up" mother has to come to terms with society and try to help it grow as well as her family. Her discussion has both experiential and intellectual elements and is aimed at encouraging mothers to be "in process" along with their children so they can grow together into mature people who define themselves, rather than adopting cardboard, ready-made images.

Notes

CHAPTER 1: RECOVERING FROM THE BIRTH

1. Alan F. Guttmacher, *Pregnancy, Birth and Family Planning* (New York: New American Library, Signet, 1937, 1947, 1950, 1956, 1962, 1965, 1973), p. 264.
2. Nicholson J. Eastman and Louis Hellman, *Williams Obstetrics*, 13th ed. (New York: Appleton-Century-Crofts, 1966), p. 479.
3. Guttmacher, *Pregnancy*, p. 265.
4. J. J. Nel, "Episiotomy," in *Episiotomy: Physical and Emotional Aspects*, Sheila Kitzinger, ed. (London: National Childbirth Trust, 9, Queensborough Terrace, n.d.), p. 16.
5. *Ibid.*, p. 16.
6. Robert E. Hall, *Nine Months' Reading* (New York: Bantam, in arrangement with Doubleday, 1960, 1963, 1972), p. 127.
7. Boston Children's Medical Center, *Pregnancy, Birth and the Newborn Baby* (New York: Delacorte, Seymour Lawrence, 1971, 1972), pp. 215–216.
8. Hall, *Nine Months' Reading*, p. 154.
9. Guttmacher, *Pregnancy*, p. 266.
10. *Ibid.*, p. 269.
11. Boston Children's Medical Center, *Pregnancy*, p. 220.
12. Guttmacher, *Pregnancy*, p. 261.
13. Boston Children's Medical Center, *Pregnancy*, pp. 209–211.
14. *Ibid.*, p. 211.
15. *Ibid.*, p. 211.

CHAPTER 2: TAKING CARE OF YOUR BABY

1. Frank Caplan, ed., *The First Twelve Months of Life* (New York: Grosset and Dunlap, 1973), p. 20.
2. U.S. Department of Health, Education and Welfare, Office of Child Development, Children's Bureau, *Infant Care* (Washington, D.C.: Superintendent of Documents, U.S. Government Printing Office, 1973), pp. 64–66.
3. Stella Chess, Alexander Thomas, and Herbert G. Birch, *Your Child Is a Person* (New York: Viking, 1965), pp. 28–32.
4. Caplan, *The First Twelve Months*, p. 28.
5. *Ibid.*, pp. 30–31.
6. *Ibid.*, p. 44.

CHAPTER 3: COPING WITH A CRYING BABY

1. Boston Children's Medical Center, *Pregnancy, Birth and the Newborn Baby* (New York: Delacorte, Seymour Lawrence, 1971, 1972), pp. 357–358.

2. T. Berry Brazelton, "Coping with a Colicky Baby," *Redbook*, Vol. 143, No. 2, June 1974, p. 72.

3. Frank Caplan, ed., *The First Twelve Months of Life* (New York: Grosset and Dunlap, 1973), p. 44.

4. Benjamin Spock, *Baby and Child Care* (New York: Pocket Books, 1968), p. 185.

5. Caplan, *The First Twelve Months*, p. 44.

6. Silvia Bell and Mary Ainsworth, "Infant Crying and Maternal Responsiveness," *Child Development*, vol. 43, no. 4, December 1972, p. 1187.

7. Spock, *Baby and Child Care*, p. 190.

8. Brazelton, "Coping with a Colicky Baby," p. 70.

9. *Ibid.*, p. 72.

10. *Ibid.*, p. 72.

11. Barbara W. Wyden, "The Difficult Baby Was Born That Way," *New York Times Magazine*, March 21, 1971, p. 67.

12. Stella Chess, Alexander Thomas, and Herbert G. Birch, *Your Child Is a Person* (New York: Viking, 1965), p. 123.

13. *Ibid.*, pp. 125–126.

14. Spock, *Baby and Child Care*, pp. 190–191.

CHAPTER 4: THE BREAST-FEEDING DECISION

1. Stella Chess, Alexander Thomas, and Herbert G. Birch, *Your Child Is a Person* (New York: Viking, 1965), pp. 62–63.

2. Marvin S. Eiger and Sally Wendkos Olds, *The Complete Book of Breastfeeding* (New York: Bantam, in arrangement with Workman, 1972), p. 15.

3. Boston Children's Medical Center, *Pregnancy, Birth and the Newborn Baby* (New York: Delacorte, Seymour Lawrence, 1971, 1972) (Hereafter *Newborn Baby*), p. 303.

4. *Ibid.*, p. 304.

5. Eiger and Olds, pp. 9–10; *Newborn Baby*, p. 304.

6. *Newborn Baby*, pp. 303–304.

7. Eiger and Olds, p. 10.

8. Alice Gerard, *Please Breast Feed Your Baby* (New York: New American Library, Signet, 1970), p. 21.

9. Sally Wendkos Olds, "In Praise of Breast-feeding," *Ms.*, vol. 1, no. 10, April 1973, p. 12.

10. *Ibid.*, p. 10.

11. Eiger and Olds, p. 57.

12. Karen Pryor, *Nursing Your Baby* (New York: Pocket Books, 1973), p. 155; Eiger and Olds, pp. 65–66.

13. Eiger and Olds, p. 88.

14. *Ibid.*, p. 98.

15. *Ibid.*, p. 105.

16. *Newborn Baby*, p. 303.

17. *Ibid.*, p. 292.

18. Gerard, p. 87.

19. *Newborn Baby*, p. 292.

20. Gerard, pp. 79–80.

21. Pryor, pp. 184–185.

22. *Ibid.*, p. 28.
23. *Ibid.*, p. 29.
24. Pryor, p. 28.; *Newborn Baby*, pp. 305–306; Eiger and Olds, p. 43.
25. Eiger and Olds, p. 44.
26. *Ibid.*, p. 107.
27. Gerard, p. 54; Pryor, p. 186; Eiger and Olds, p. 106.
28. Benjamin Spock, *Baby and Child Care* (New York: Pocket Books, 1968), p. 95.
29. Pryor, p. 163.
30. Eiger and Olds, p. 148.
31. *Ibid.*, pp. 148–149.
32. *Ibid.*, p. 150.
33. Pryor, pp. 204–206; Eiger and Olds, pp. 152–153.
34. Eiger and Olds, p. 152.
35. Eiger and Olds, p. 152.
36. Alan F. Guttmacher, *Pregnancy, Birth and Family Planning* (New York: New American Library, Signet, 1937, 1947, 1950, 1956, 1962, 1965, 1973), p. 277.
37. Gerard, p. 91; Eiger and Olds, p. 152.
38. Eiger and Olds, p. 153.
39. Pryor, p. 206; Eiger and Olds, p. 153.
40. Pryor, p. 211.
41. *Ibid.*, p. 212.
42. Olds, "In Praise of Breast-feeding," p. 13.
43. Spock, *Baby and Child Care*, p. 91.
44. Spock, pp. 100–103; Pryor, p. 220.
45. Eiger and Olds, p. 166.
46. *Ibid.*, p. 175.
47. *Ibid.*, p. 175.
48. Pryor, p. 248.
49. Eiger and Olds, pp. 188–189.
50. *Ibid.*, p. 191

CHAPTER 5: RE-ESTABLISHING CLOSENESS AS A COUPLE

1. Sheila Kitzinger, *Giving Birth: The Parents Emotions in Childbirth* (New York: Taplinger Pub. Co., 1971), p. 30.
2. Fred Belliveau and Lin Richter, *Understanding Human Sexual Inadequacy* (New York: Bantam, by arrangement with Little, Brown and Co., 1970), pp. 104–105.
3. Carl Rogers, *Becoming Partners: Marriage and Its Alternatives* (New York: Delacorte, 1972), p. 61.
4. Boston Women's Health Book Collective, *Our Bodies, Ourselves* (New York: Simon and Schuster, 1971, 1973) (Hereafter, *Our Bodies*), p. 221; William H. Masters and Virginia E. Johnson, *Human Sexual Response.* (Boston: Little, Brown and Co., 1966), p. 150.
5. Belliveau and Richter, *Understanding Inadequacy*, p. 201.
6. *Ibid.*, p. 196.

7. *Our Bodies*, p. 222; Masters and Johnson, *Response*, pp. 150–151.
8. Sheila Kitzinger, *The Experience of Childbirth* (Baltimore: Penguin, Pelican, 1962, 1967, 1972), p. 254.
9. Karen Pryor, *Nursing Your Baby* (New York: Pocket Books, 1973), p. 221.
10. Ruth and Edward Brecher, eds., *An Analysis of Human Sexual Response* (New York: New American Library, Signet, 1966), p. 91; Masters and Johnson, *Response*, pp. 161–162.
11. Donna Cherniak and Allan Feingold, *Birth Control Handbook*, 11th ed., (Montreal: Montreal Health Press, 1973) (Hereafter, *Birth Control Handbook*), p. 18.
12. *Our Bodies*, p. 113.
13. *Birth Control Handbook*, p. 23.
14. *Our Bodies*, pp. 115–116.
15. Judith Ramsey, "The Modern Woman's Guide to Her Own Body," *Family Circle*, vol. 83, no. 1, July 1973, p. 115.
16. *Our Bodies*, pp. 116–119; *Birth Control Handbook*, pp. 21–22.
17. *Birth Control Handbook*, p. 27.
18. *Ibid.*, p. 29.
19. Alan Guttmacher, *Pregnancy, Birth and Family Planning* (New York: New American Library, Signet, 1937, 1947, 1950, 1956, 1962, 1965, 1973), p. 316.
20. Ramsey, "The Modern Woman's Guide," p. 116; Guttmacher, *Pregnancy*, p. 316; *Our Bodies*, p. 120.
21. *Birth Control Handbook*, p. 27; *Our Bodies*, p. 121.
22. *Birth Control Handbook*, p. 29.
23. *Ibid.*, p. 29.
24. *Ibid.*, p. 30.
25. *Birth Control Handbook*, p. 30; Guttmacher, *Pregnancy*, p. 318.
26. *Birth Control Handbook*, p. 30.
27. *Our Bodies*, p. 121.
28. Guttmacher, *Pregnancy*, p. 317.
29. Lynn K. Hansen, Barbara Reskin, and Diana Gray, *How to Have Intercourse Without Getting Screwed* (Seattle: Associated Students of the University of Washington Women's Commission, 1972), p. 11.
30. *Birth Control Handbook*, p. 33; *Our Bodies*, pp. 125–126.
31. *Our Bodies*, pp. 125–126.
32. *Our Bodies*, p. 126; *Birth Control Handbook*, p. 34.
33. Guttmacher, *Pregnancy*, p. 324.
34. *Our Bodies*, p. 128; Hansen, *How to Have Intercourse*, p. 12.
35. *Birth Control Handbook*, p. 32.
36. *Our Bodies*, p. 130.
37. *Ibid.*, p. 130.
38. *Our Bodies*, p. 128; Hansen, *How to Have Intercourse*, p. 12.
39. *Birth Control Handbook*, p. 35.
40. *Our Bodies*, p. 132.
41. *Ibid.*, pp. 132–133.
42. *Birth Control Handbook*, p. 40.
43. *Our Bodies*, p. 136.
44. Guttmacher, *Pregnancy*, p. 335.
45. *Ibid.*, p. 342.
46. *Birth Control Handbook*, pp. 39–40.

CHAPTER 6: FEELING COMFORTABLE AS PARENTS

1. Angela Barron McBride, *The Growth and Development of Mothers* (New York: Harper and Row, 1973), p. 49.
2. Boston Women's Health Book Collective, *Our Bodies, Ourselves* (New York: Simon and Schuster, 1971, 1973), pp. 215–16.
3. *Ibid.*, p. 217.

Glossary

Afterpains. Abdominal cramps felt for several days after giving birth, caused by contractions of the uterus as it shrinks to its non-pregnant size. Likely to be more noticeable after the second or third child than after the first.

Basal body temperature thermometer. A thermometer that registers only a few degrees, from 96°F. to 100°F. with 1/10 degree gradations. Used for measuring a woman's temperature to determine when she is ovulating.

Breech. Baby is in such a position in the uterus that her buttocks have to be delivered first.

Catheterization. Procedure whereby urine is emptied from the bladder by inserting a small pliable tube through the urethra into the bladder.

Cervix. The narrow, neck-like, lower end of the uterus; opens into the vagina.

Cesarean section. Delivery of the baby by means of an incision into the uterus through the abdominal wall. Also called C-section.

Colostrum. The thin, yellow fluid secreted by the breasts during the first few days after delivery (and sometimes during pregnancy as well). Is the forerunner of breast milk, believed to be rich in protein and immunity-granting substances.

Douche. Flushing out the vagina with a stream of water sometimes mixed with a special solution. Douching is seldom a medical necessity and as a routine procedure can even be dangerous, particularly during pregnancy and the postpartum period. Douche only when specifically recommended by the doctor, and do not expect douching after intercourse to be an effective way of preventing conception.

Ejaculate. To discharge semen suddenly and rhythmically from the penis at the time of orgasm.

Engorgement. The condition of extreme fullness of the breasts as a result of an increased flow of blood and/or milk into that area.

Episiotomy. An incision made in the area between the vagina and the rectum prior to delivery for the purpose of easing the baby's passage by widening the outlet; done to prevent tearing of the tissues during childbirth.

Estrogen. The hormone secreted by the ovaries which is essential to the development of the lining of the uterus and feminization of the body.

Fallopian tubes. The two small tubes that extend from the uterus to the ovaries. When an egg (ovum) is expelled from an ovary it goes into a Fallopian tube where it is either fertilized or passed on through into the uterus and on out of the body.

Hemorrhoids. Dilated veins under the skin of the anus; also called piles. Often develop during pregnancy or at the time of delivery.

Hormone. Any of various chemical substances which are secreted by endocrine glands and which travel through the bloodstream to specific parts of the body. Hormones influence basic growth processes and sexual development, as well as personality characteristics. Menstruation, conception, pregnancy, and lactation are all dependent on hormones.

i.v. Intravenous. Sterile fluids are sometimes introduced into the veins for nutrition, hydration, or medication, during delivery or soon after.

Kegel exercise. Tightening the muscles of the anus, vagina, and urethra to restore muscle tone to that area.

Lactation. The secretion of milk by the breasts; under the control of hormones.

Let-down reflex. The squeezing out of milk from the sacs where it is produced into the ducts where it then becomes available to the baby through the nipple; often accompanied by a tingling sensation in the breasts.

Lochia. Vaginal discharge of blood, mucus, and tissue that continues for three to six weeks after childbirth, gradually changing in color from a bright red to pink and then to almost white.

Mastitis. Localized inflammation of the breast, usually during the first month after childbirth. Fever, flu-like aching and chills, and tenderness in one breast are the usual symptoms. If untreated, a serious abcess is likely to develop.

Nipple shield. A rubber nipple attached to a cone that can be placed over the front of the breast if the mother's nipple becomes cracked. As the baby sucks on the rubber nipple, a vacuum is created in the cone and milk is drawn out of the breast. Filling the shield halfway with water may eliminate the discomfort to the breast that might otherwise occur as the baby sucks.

Orgasm. A complex series of responses involving rhythmic contractions of the genital organs and the intense and pleasurable release of tension throughout the body; also referred to as the climax of intercourse.

Ovary. One of the pair of female glands of reproduction in which the egg (ovum) develops each month.

Ovulation. The monthly release of an egg from the ovary; precedes menstruation by two weeks.

Oxytocin. The hormone produced by the pituitary gland that causes the uterus to contract and also causes the cells around the milk-producing sacs to contract, thereby squeezing the milk out into the ducts where the baby can get it. Also available in nasal spray and tablet form for special circumstances in which a nursing mother is having difficulty letting down her milk. Also called the let-down hormone.

Pelvic floor. The group of muscles that support the rectum, urethra, and bladder, as well as the internal reproductive organs.

Perineum. The external tissues between the vagina and rectum.

Placenta. The organ developed during pregnancy through which the baby derives oxygen and nourishment and excretes wastes; also called "afterbirth." Is delivered immediately after the baby.

Postpartum. After delivery; following childbirth.

Progesterone. The hormone secreted by the ovary after ovulation which is responsible for preparing the lining of the uterus for the fertilized egg; essential to maintaining a pregnancy.

Rooming-in. An arrangement offered by some hospitals in which the baby and mother are in the same room much of the time so that the mother can care for her child.

"Safe period." The time during the month when it is relatively "safe" to have intercourse without getting pregnant—specifically, the first week of the menstrual cycle (including menstruation) and the last week of the cycle

(the week preceding menstruation). Women whose monthly periods are irregular and unpredictable can only be sure of the safety of the first week.

Scrotum. The pouch of skin that contains two testicles, located behind the penis.

Semen. The impregnating fluid produced by male reproductive organs, containing sperm.

Sitz bath. A very shallow bath, usually involving a special container that fits over a toilet seat. An attached bag of hot water serves to maintain a soothingly hot temperature. Helps cleanse, soothe, and heal the area that is sore after giving birth (including both the episiotomy and hemorrhoids).

Sperm. Male reproductive cells, produced in the testicles.

Spermicidal. Sperm-killing.

Stretch marks. Marks that sometimes develop during pregnancy as the skin is stretched to make room for the growing fetus, usually in the abdominal area but sometimes on the breasts as well. After delivery the stretch marks gradually become less noticeable.

Testicles. The two male sex glands located in the scrotum where sperm are produced.

Transverse. Crosswise position of the baby in the uterus in which a shoulder or occasionally an arm and hand are in the pelvis, instead of the head. Vaginal delivery is impossible when the baby is in this position, so a Cesarean section must be performed unless the infant can be turned by the doctor before the delivery.

Umbilical cord. A cord about one half inch in diameter and about twenty inches long, containing blood vessels and extending from the navel of the baby to the inside surface of the placenta. Once tied, immediately after delivery, its stump gradually dries up and falls off, usually by the end of the third week.

Urethra. The tube which carries the urine from the bladder to the outside of the body.

Uterus. Womb; the muscular organ, normally the size of a pear, in which a fertilized egg develops into a baby; also the source of menstruation.

Vagina. Birth canal; the very elastic, curved canal extending from the uterus to the outside of the body; lubricates, expands, and contracts during intercourse.

Vaginal suppositories. Contraceptives with a soap, gelatine, or cocoa-butter base that are solid at ordinary temperatures but melt when inserted into the vagina. Must be in place a few minutes prior to intercourse, but are only effective for an hour or so after insertion. A very unreliable method of birth control.

Varicose veins. Abnormally swollen or dilated veins that develop on a woman's legs during pregnancy. Heredity seems to play a role in the development of varicose veins, and the problem often increases with each successive pregnancy.

Venereal disease. Bacterial infections, such as gonorrhea or syphilis, that are acquired through sexual contact with another person who has the disease.

Bibliography

CHAPTER 1: RECOVERING FROM THE BIRTH

Boston Children's Medical Center. *Pregnancy, Birth and the Newborn Baby.* New York: Delacorte, Seymour Lawrence, 1971, 1972.

Boston Women's Health Book Collective. *Our Bodies, Ourselves.* New York: Simon and Schuster, 1971, 1973.

Eastman, Nicholson J., and Louis Hellman. *Williams Obstetrics.* 13th ed., New York: Appleton-Century-Crofts, 1966.

Guttmacher, Alan F. *Pregnancy, Birth and Family Planning.* New York: New American Library, Signet, 1937, 1947, 1950, 1956, 1962, 1965, 1973.

Hall, Robert E. *Nine Months' Reading.* New York: Bantam, in arrangement with Doubleday, 1960, 1963, 1972.

Kitzinger, Sheila, ed. *Episiotomy: Physical and Emotional Aspects.* London: National Childbirth Trust, 9, Queensborough Terrace, n.d.

U.S. Department of Health, Education and Welfare, Office of Child Development, Children's Bureau. *Prenatal Care.* Washington, D.C.: Superintendent of Documents, U.S. Government Printing Office, 1973. DHEW Publication No. (OCD) 73–17. $.75.

Willson, J. Robert; Beecham, Clayton T.; Carrington, Elsie Reid. *Obstetrics and Gynecology.* 4th ed., St. Louis: C.V. Mosby, 1971.

CHAPTER 2: TAKING CARE OF YOUR BABY

Aston, Athina. *How to Play with Your Baby.* New York: The Learning Child, 1971.

Boston Children's Medical Center. *Pregnancy, Birth and the Newborn Baby.* New York: Delacorte, Seymour Lawrence, 1971, 1972.

Brazelton, T. Berry. *Infants and Mothers.* New York: Delta, Dell, Delacorte Press, Seymour Lawrence, 1969.

Caplan, Frank, ed. *The First Twelve Months of Life.* New York: Grosset and Dunlap, 1973, originally published as 12 booklets in 1971, 1972, by Edcom Systems, Princeton, N.J.

Chess, Stella; Thomas, Alexander; and Birch, Herbert G. *Your Child Is a Person.* New York: Viking Press, Viking Compass Ed., 1965.

Dodson, Fitzhugh. *How to Father.* Los Angeles: Nash, 1974.

Dodson, Fitzhugh. *How to Parent.* New York: New American Library, Signet, 1970.

Fraiberg, Selma. *The Magic Years.* New York: Charles Scribner's Sons, 1959.

Gordon, Ira J., *Baby Learning Through Baby Play.* New York: St. Martin's, 1970.

Newton, Niles. *The Family Book of Child Care.* New York: Harper and Row, 1967.

Spock, Benjamin. *Baby and Child Care.* New York: Pocket Books, 1945, 1946, 1957, 1968.

U.S. Department of Health, Education and Welfare, Office of Child Development, Children's Bureau. *Infant Care.* Washington, D.C.: Superintendent of Documents, U.S. Government Printing Office, 1973. DHEW Publication No. (OCD) 73–15.

U.S. Department of Health, Education and Welfare, Office of Child Development, Children's Bureau, *Your Child From 1 to 6.* Washington, D.C.: Superintendent of Documents, U.S. Government Printing Office, 1962. DHEW Publication No. (OCD) 73–26.

CHAPTER 3: COPING WITH A CRYING BABY

Bell, Silvia M., and Ainsworth, Mary D. Salter. "Infant Crying and Maternal Responsiveness." *Child Development.* Vol. 43, no. 4, December 1972, pp. 1171–1190.

Boston Children's Medical Center. *Pregnancy, Birth and the Newborn Baby.* New York: Delacorte, Seymour Lawrence, 1971, 1972.

Brazelton, T. Berry. "Coping with a Colicky Baby." *Redbook.* Vol. 143, no. 2, June 1974, pp. 70–72.

Caplan, Frank, ed. *The First Twelve Months of Life.* New York: Grosset and Dunlap, 1973, originally published as 12 booklets in 1971, 1972, by Edcom Systems, Princeton, N.J.

Chess, Stella; Thomas, Alexander; and Birch, Herbert G. *Your Child Is a Person.* New York: Viking Press. Viking Compass Ed., 1965.

Spock, Benjamin. *Baby and Child Care.* New York: Pocket Books, 1945, 1946, 1957, 1968.

Wyden, Barbara W. "The Difficult Baby Is Born That Way." *New York Times Magazine.* March 21, 1971, pp. 67+.

U.S. Department of Health, Education and Welfare, Office of Child Development, Children's Bureau. *Infant Care.* Washington, D.C.: Superintendent of Documents, U.S. Government Printing Office, 1973. DHEW Publication No. (OCD) 73–15.

CHAPTER 4: THE BREAST-FEEDING DECISION

Boston Children's Medical Center. *Pregnancy, Birth and the Newborn Baby.* New York: Delacorte, Seymour Lawrence, 1971, 1972.

Chess, Stella; Thomas, Alexander; and Birch, Herbert G. *Your Child Is a Person.* New York: Viking Press, Viking Compass Ed., 1965.

Eiger, Marvin S., and Olds, Sally Wendkos. *The Complete Book of Breastfeeding.* New York: Bantam, in arrangement with Workman, 1972.

Gerard, Alice. *Please Breast Feed Your Baby.* New York: New American Library, Signet, 1970.

Guttmacher, Alan F. *Pregnancy, Birth and Family Planning.* New York: New American Library, Signet, 1937, 1947, 1950, 1956, 1962, 1965, 1973.

La Leche League International. *The Womanly Art of Breast-feeding.* Franklin Park, Ill.: La Leche League International, 1958, 1963.

Olds, Sally Wendkos. "In Praise of Breast-feeding." *Ms.* Vol. 1, No. 10, April 1973.

Pryor, Karen. *Nursing Your Baby.* New York: Pocket Books, 1973.

Spock, Benjamin. *Baby and Child Care.* New York: Pocket Books, 1945, 1946, 1957, 1968.

CHAPTER 5: RE-ESTABLISHING CLOSENESS AS A COUPLE

Belliveau, Fred, and Richter, Lin. *Understanding Human Sexual Inadequacy.* New York: Bantam, published in arrangement with Little, Brown and Co., 1970.
Boston Women's Health Book Collective. *Our Bodies, Ourselves.* New York: Simon and Schuster, 1971, 1973.
Brecher, Ruth, and Brecher, Howard, eds. *An Analysis of Human Sexual Response.* New York: New American Library, Signet, 1966.
Brody, Jan E. "A Complete Guide to Birth Control Today." *Woman's Day.* September, 1973, pp. 50+.
Cherniak, Donna, and Feingold, Allan. *Birth Control Handbook.* 11th ed., Montreal: Montreal Health Press, 1973.
Guttmacher, Alan F. *Pregnancy, Birth and Family Planning.* New York: New American Library, Signet, 1937, 1947, 1950, 1956, 1962, 1965, 1973.
Hansen, Lynn K.; Reskin, Barbara; and Gray, Diana. *How To Have Intercourse Without Getting Screwed.* Seattle: Associated Students of the University of Washington Women's Commission, 1972.
Kitzinger, Sheila. *Giving Birth: The Parents' Emotions in Childbirth.* New York: Taplinger Pub. Co., 1971.
Kitzinger, Sheila. *The Experience of Childbirth.* Baltimore: Penguin, Pelican. 1962, 1967, 1972.
Masters, William H., and Johnson, Virginia E. *Human Sexual Inadequacy.* Boston: Little, Brown and Co., 1970.
Masters, William H., and Johnson, Virginia E. *Human Sexual Response.* Boston: Little, Brown and Co., 1966.
Pryor, Karen. *Nursing Your Baby.* New York: Pocket Books, 1973.
Ramsey, Judith. "The Modern Woman's Health Guide to Her Own Body." *Family Circle.* Vol. 83, no. 1, July, 1973, pp. 113+.
Rogers, Carl. *Becoming Partners: Marriage and Its Alternatives.* New York: Delacorte, 1972.

CHAPTER 6: FEELING COMFORTABLE AS PARENTS

Boston Children's Medical Center. *Pregnancy, Birth and the Newborn Baby.* New York: Delacorte, Seymour Lawrence, 1971, 1972.
Boston Women's Health Book Collective. *Our Bodies, Ourselves.* New York: Simon and Schuster, 1971, 1973.
Chess, Stella; Thomas, Alexander; and Birch, Herbert G. *Your Child Is a Person.* New York: Viking Press, Viking Compass Ed., 1965.
McBride, Angela Barron. *The Growth and Development of Mothers.* New York: Harper and Row, 1973.

Index